MW00973082

The Best I've Ever Tasted

By Margaret J. Galbreath

The Roper Group, Inc.
Raleigh, North Carolina

Copyright © 1995 by Margaret J. Galbreath

All rights reserved. No part of this book may be reproduced in any form or by any means without permission from the Publisher.

Inquiries should be addressed to:

The Roper Group
PO Box 20573
Raleigh, NC 27619

Art work by Lisa Stockard, Beaufort NC
Book design by Jess R. McLamb, Raleigh NC
Editing by Thomas A. Galbreath, Kinston NC
Jess R. McLamb and Charlotte A. Ranz, Raleigh NC

Additional copies may be ordered by calling (919) 782-8956

ISBN 0-9645096-2-8

The Roper Group
Raleigh, North Carolina 27619-0573

Printed in the United States of America

The Best I've Ever Tasted

Acknowledgments

This book would not be possible had it not been for several special people in my life...

My devoted friends, Cora Davis and her sister, Aver Lee Simmons, former chefs at the Kinston, North Carolina Country Club. We experimented together and created what we thought were masterpieces.

My grandmother, Liza Wooten, for her infinite patience through my very young years.

My mother, Helen Jones (she was always delighted when I got in the kitchen and she didn't have to).

My daughter, Jess McLamb, who spent many hours at the computer and cracked the whip to motivate me to complete this book ... bless her!

And, of course, husband Tom, for his help in proofing and his joy of good food (which came from having his mother, Amine, who was a wonderful cook).

Last, but not least, a host of friends who encouraged me to write this book and contributed many of the recipes (see next page).

Contributors

Contents

Appetizers and Pickles

Bacon and Cream Cheese Toast

This is a favorite of my youngest daughter, Liza Franklin, from Raleigh (NC). She says it's best when served hot.

1   **pound bacon**
1   **container cream cheese with chives, softened**
1   **loaf whole wheat bread**

Preheat oven to 400 degrees.

Cut bacon into thirds. Cut crusts off all slices of bread and then cut each slice of bread into four pieces. Spread bread with cream cheese. Roll bread pieces (cream cheese is inside the roll) and wrap with bacon. Secure each roll with a toothpick and place on an ungreased cookie sheet. Continue until all bacon is used.

Bake in the oven until bacon is brown and crispy and the edges of the bread are brown as well.

Serves 6 to 8.

Oriental Cashew Crunch

The more you eat, the more you want!

1	package (8 cups) oat cereal
1	can (3 ounces or 1 1/2 cups) chow mein noodles
1	cup cashews or pecans
1/3	cup vegetable oil
3	tablespoons soy sauce
1	teaspoon garlic powder
1	teaspoon onion powder

Preheat oven to 250 degrees.

Combine cereal, noodles, and nuts in a 13" x 9" pan. Set aside.

Combine oil, soy sauce, garlic powder, and onion powder in a small mixing bowl. Pour over cereal mixture and stir to coat evenly. Bake 1 hour, stirring every 20 minutes. Cool and store in an airtight container.

Makes 10 cups.

Cheese Crackers

This is an original recipe from Hatcher Kinchloe of Rocky Mount.

40	saltine crackers
	ground red pepper
8	ounces sharp or extra sharp Cheddar cheese, coarsely grated

Place crackers side by side on an 11" x 16" non-stick coated cookie sheet, completely filling the surface. If bottom row of crackers will not fit, trim them with scissors. Crackers must fit tightly so cheese will not run between. Sprinkle crackers lightly with pepper, to taste. Place grated cheese on all crackers, as evenly as possible.

Place pan on bottom shelf of cold oven. Turn oven to broil and leave door open. After about 10 minutes, cheese will begin to bubble. The bubbles will break and get smaller in the next few minutes. When the cheese stops bubbling, remove pan from oven. Set aside while oven cools, then bake at 150 degrees for several hours or overnight to dry crackers out.

Makes 40 crackers.

Cheese Dabs

So easy to make!

1	package (8 ounces) Cracker Barrel sharp Cheddar cheese, grated
1	stick margarine, softened
1/2	teaspoon salt
1/2	teaspoon Tabasco
1/2	teaspoon paprika
1	cup all-purpose flour
1 1/2	cups crisp rice cereal

Preheat oven to 375 degrees.

Blend cheese with margarine. Add salt, Tabasco, paprika, and flour. Mix thoroughly. Gently fold in cereal. Shape mixture into small (approximately 1 inch diameter) balls.

Place balls on an ungreased cookie sheet, about 2 inches apart. Bake for 10 minutes or until brown.

Makes about 3 dozen balls.

Toasted Cheese Rounds

Amine Edwards, my sister-in-law from Rocky Mount, shared this easy to fix hors d'oeuvre.

1/4	cup grated Mozarella cheese
1/3	cup Parmesan cheese
1/3	cup Romano cheese
3/4	cup mayonnaise
1/2	cup chopped red onion
1	loaf party rye bread

Preheat oven to broil.

Combine cheeses, mayonnaise, and onion in a medium size mixing bowl. Spread mixture over rye bread slices. Place bread slices on a cookie sheet. Broil until cheese is bubbling.

Serves 4 to 6 people.

Cheese Straws

This was originally made by my mother, Helen Jones, and passed on to me.

1	pound (4 sticks) butter, softened
1	pound sharp Cheddar cheese, grated
3	cups all-purpose flour
2	teaspoons cayenne pepper
1	teaspoon salt

Preheat oven to 375 degrees.

Combine butter and cheese in a medium size bowl. Stir flour, pepper and salt into the cheese mixture. Blend thoroughly with a pastry blender or fork. Squeeze through cookie press or shape into balls.

Place on a lightly greased cookie sheet, one inch apart. Bake for 10 minutes or until golden brown. Cool on wire rack. Place in an airtight container. These stay fresh for several weeks.

Makes 10 to 12 dozen.

Cheese Wafers

Just delicious! Store in an airtight container (don't freeze) and enjoy for at least two weeks.

2	cups shredded sharp Cheddar cheese
1/2	cup butter, softened
1/2	teaspoon cayenne pepper
1/2	teaspoon dry mustard
1	cup all-purpose flour
2	cups crisp rice cereal
3	dozen pecan halves
	confectioners' sugar

Preheat oven to 350 degrees.

Combine cheese and butter. Cream until smooth using an electric mixture. Add pepper, mustard and flour and mix well. Stir in cereal.

Form dough into small balls, then flatten ball with a fork to make a wafer. Place a pecan half on the wafer and place wafer on a lightly greased cookie sheet. Bake for 12 to 15 minutes or until lightly brown. Cool, then dust with sugar.

Makes about 3 dozen.

Ranch Oyster Crackers

These keep for several weeks in an airtight container.

5	cups plain oyster crackers
1	package (1 ounce) Ranch salad dressing mix
1/2	teaspoon dill weed
3/4	cup salad oil
1/4	teaspoon lemon pepper, optional
1/4	teaspoon garlic powder, optional

Preheat oven to 250 degrees.

Place crackers in a large bowl. Set aside.

Combine salad dressing mix with dill weed and oil. Add lemon pepper and garlic powder, if desired. Pour over crackers and stir well to be sure all crackers are coated. Place crackers in a roasting pan and bake for 15 to 20 minutes, stirring occasionally.

Makes 5 cups.

Spicy Party Mix

Give a jar for Christmas!

3/4	pound (3 sticks) butter or margarine, melted
1	tablespoon garlic salt
1	tablespoon celery salt
1/2	teaspoon ground red pepper
2	tablespoons Worchestershire sauce
1	box (16 ounces) rice cereal
1	box (16 ounces) wheat cereal
1	box (16 ounces) corn cereal
1	bag (10 ounces) pretzel sticks
3	cups salted peanuts or pecans

Preheat oven to 250 degrees.

Stir garlic salt, celery salt, red pepper and Worchestershire sauce into butter. Place cereals, pretzels and nuts in a large roasting pan. Pour butter mixture over, and stir to coat.

Bake slowly for 60 minutes, stirring occasionally. Cool and store in an airtight container.

Makes about 8 cups.

Hot Crabmeat Canapes

These are elegant! Suggest using rye bread rounds.

1/2	pound crabmeat
6	tablespoons mayonnaise
1/2	teaspoon salt
1/2	teaspoon MSG (optional)
1	tablespoon grated onion
1	teaspoon fresh lemon juice
1/2	cup Parmesan cheese
36	small rounds bread (size of a silver dollar)
	paprika

Preheat oven to broil.

Combine crabmeat, mayonnaise, salt, MSG, onion, lemon juice and cheese. Mix well. Spread on bread rounds. Sprinkle with paprika. Place bread rounds on a cookie sheet. Broil until bubbling and lightly browned. Serve immediately.

Makes 36.

Baked Brie

This is great hors d'oeuvre with cocktails.

1/2   **cup coarsely chopped pecans**
1   **tablespoon butter or margarine, melted**
1   **wheel (1 pound) baby brie cheese**
1/4   **cup dark brown sugar**

Preheat oven to 300 degrees.

Place pecans on small pan. Pour butter over pecans and stir until well coated. Toast pecans for about 10 minutes, stirring occasionally.

Place brie in a small pie pan. Cover the top of the brie with brown sugar. Sprinkle toasted pecans over sugar. Bake brie at 325 degrees for about 15 minutes. Serve immediately with bland crackers.

Serves 8.

Cheddar Cheese Ball

Aunt Jess Heller from New Milford (CT) loved this!

1	pound sharp Cheddar cheese, grated
1	package (8 ounces) cream cheese, softened
8	ounces Roquefort or Blue cheese, softened
1	medium white onion, grated
3	teaspoons Worchestershire sauce
1	teaspoon Texas Pete hot sauce
3/4	cup finely chopped fresh parsley or pecans

Combine all three cheeses in a medium size mixing bowl. Add onion, Worchestershire sauce and hot sauce and mix until all ingredients are well blended. Cover and refrigerate 1 hour.

Form into a ball and roll in either the parsley or the pecans. Serve with crackers or melba rounds.

Serves approximately 20.

Cheese Spread

Mimi Parrott from Salisbury (NC) shared this.

1	**package (8 ounces) cream cheese, softened**
3/4	**cup chopped almonds**
1/4	**cup chopped onions**
3	**tablespoons chopped pimentos**
1	**tablespoon catsup**
1/2	**teaspoon salt or to taste**
1/2	**teaspoon pepper or to taste**

Combine all ingredients in a small mixing bowl and blend well. Press into a crock or serving dish. Cover and refrigerate before serving. Serve with crackers.

Serves 6.

Hot Crabmeat Cocktail Spread

You can prepare the spread ahead of time and bake just before serving.

1	package (8 ounces) cream cheese, softened
1	tablespoon milk
1/2	pound crabmeat
2	tablespoons chopped onion
2	tablespoons toasted slivered almonds
2	teaspoons Worchestershire sauce
	toast rounds (alternative)

Preheat oven to 350 degrees.

Thoroughly combine cheese and milk in a medium size mixing bowl. Add crabmeat, onion and almonds.Place mixture in a greased 1-quart casserole dish. Bake until bubbly.

Alternative: Spread on toast rounds, then bake.

Serves 6.

Shrimp and Cheese Spread

This spread is great served with Triscuits.

2	cups finely chopped shrimp, lobster, or crabmeat
2	packages (8 ounces each) cream cheese, softened
1	small wedge (3 to 4 ounces) Roquefort cheese
1/4	pound sharp Cheddar cheese, grated
1	tablespoon Worshestershire sauce
1	tablespoon mayonnaise
1	tablespoon lemon juice
1	tablespoon garlic salt
1	teaspoon paprika
	salt to taste
	salad oil (enough to oil mold)

Combine all ingredients in a blender or food processor and blend well. Press mixture firmly into an oiled 1-quart mold. Refrigerate overnight. Unmold onto a serving platter.

Serves 20.

Salmon Ball

Another favorite from Aunt Jess Heller of New Milford (CT).

1	can (1 pound) red salmon
1	package (8 ounces) cream cheese, softened
2	tablespoons lemon juice
3	teaspoons grated onion
2	teaspoons horseradish
1/2	teaspoon salt
	dash of Worchestershire sauce
	several dashes of ground red pepper to taste
1/4	teaspoon liquid smoke (very important to include)
1/2	cup chopped pecans
3	tablespoons minced parsley

Drain salmon, then remove skin, bones, and flake with a fork. Combine salmon, cheese, lemon juice, onion, horseradish, Worchestershire sauce, and red pepper in a small mixing bowl, using an electric mixer.

Chill for 1 hour, then form into a ball. Combine pecans and parsley on wax paper and spead evenly on paper. Roll salmon ball in pecans and parsley until well coated.

Serves 8 to 10.

Salmon or Shrimp Mousse

Rich and wonderful!

1	can condensed tomato soup
	milk (fill soup can)
3	small packages (4 ounces each) cream cheese, softened
2	envelopes unflavored gelatin
1/3	cup chopped onion
1/3	cup chopped green pepper
	dash of Worchestershire sauce
	dash of Tabasco sauce
1/3	cup chopped celery
2	pounds cleaned shrimp or 2 cups red salmon, drained
	salt and pepper to taste
1	cup mayonnaise
1	cup finely chopped cucumber

Heat soup and milk in a medium sauce pan. Take pan off the stove and add cheese. Beat until smooth. Dissolve gelatin in 1/2 cup cold water. Stir gelatin into hot cheese mixture. Add onion, green pepper, Worchestershire sauce, Tabasco sauce, celery, seafood, salt and pepper to cheese mixture.

Pour into a 1-quart mold and chill 4 hours or until set. Unmold on a serving platter. Mix mayonnaise and cucumber and place on top of mold. Serve with melba toast or crackers.

Serves 25 people.

Dilled Salmon Mousse

A little trouble - but worth it!

1	can (16 ounces) red salmon
3	small scallions (with some of the green)
1	cucumber, peeled and seeded
4	ounces cream cheese, softened
2	envelopes unflavored gelatin
1/2	cup dry white wine
1/2	cup V-8 juice
2	tablespoons fresh dill or 2 teaspoons dried (to taste)
2	tablespoons cognac or brandy
	Tabasco sauce to taste
	freshly ground white pepper and salt to taste
	nutmeg to taste
1/2	cup heavy cream, whipped
1/2	cup sour cream

Drain salmon and reserve juice. Remove any dark skin and bones. Mince scallions in a food processor or blender. Add salmon, cucumber and cream cheese and puree until smooth.

Dissolve gelatin in white wine. In an enameled saucepan, heat V-8 juice, salmon juice, and wine/gelatin mixture to boiling. Simmer about 1 minute, stirring occasionally. Add to salmon puree and blend or process well. Add dill, cognac, Tabasco, salt, pepper and nutmeg and blend until mixture is light and fluffy. Chill, stirring occasionally, until thick and almost set.

Whip cream and add to salmon mixture along with sour cream. Fold all ingredients together well. Taste to correct seasoning. Pour into a 6-cup fish or seafood mold and chill for 5 hours or until set. Unmold on a serving platter. Serve with melba toast or crackers.

Serves about 12 people.

Braunschweiger Pate

You'll love this pate with cocktails before dinner. Be sure to freeze leftovers for the next get-together!

1	pound braunschweiger
2	packages green onion dip mix
1	teaspoon sugar
1 to 2	tablespoons brandy (optional)
2	packages (3 ounce) cream cheese, softened
1	tablespoon milk
1/8	teaspoon Tabasco sauce
1	teaspoon garlic salt

Mash braunschweiger in a blender. Combine dip mix, sugar, brandy, and 2 teaspoons of water to braunschweiger and blend. Form mixture into an igloo shape and place on the serving plate.

Whip cream cheese with milk and Tabasco. Blend in garlic salt. Spread cream cheese mixture over braunschweiger. Chill. Garnish with parsley and serve with crackers.

Serves 6 to 8.

Chicken Liver Pate

This came from Jerry Siegler, from Kinston (NC), who has shared many wonderful recipes with me!

6	tablespoons butter or margarine, softened
2	medium onions, diced
2	cloves garlic, finely minced
2	scallions, finely chopped
1	pound chicken livers, washed
2	teaspoons unflavored gelatin
1/2	cup chicken broth, heated to boiling
1	tablespoon finely chopped parsley
1/2	cup Port wine
1	teaspoon salt
1/2	teaspoon crushed thyme
1/2	teaspoon tarragon
1/4	teaspoon ground nutmeg
	ground pepper to taste
	parsley and pimento for garnish

Melt 3 tablespoons of butter in a skillet. Add onions, garlic, and scallions and saute until tender. Add chicken livers. Cook until the livers lose their bright color and become firm. Remove from heat.

In a small bowl, soften gelatin in 2 tablespoons cold water. Add broth. Stir until gelatin is dissolved. Pour into blender. Add liver mixture, parsley, wine, and spices to blender. Blend at medium speed until mixture is smooth. Add remaining butter, one tablespoon at a time, until well blended. Place in a crock or serving bowl. Garnish with parsley and pimento. Cover and chill for 4 hours. Will keep in the refrigerator for 2 or 3 days and will freeze well up to one month.

Serves 8 to 10.

Tuna Pate

Here's a delicious pate for tuna lovers ...

1	**package (8 ounces) cream cheese, softened**
2	**tablespoons chili sauce**
2	**tablespoons chopped parsley**
1	**teaspoon instant minced onions**
1/2	**teaspoon Tabasco sauce**
2	**cans (6 or 7 ounce) tuna, drained**

Mix all ingredients together in a blender at medium speed until smooth. Pack into a 4-cup mold. Chill at least 3 hours. Unmold and serve with crackers.

Serves 6 to 8.

Hot Artichoke Dip

Sue Lawson from Kinston shared this version of the popular artichoke dip.

2	cans (20 ounces) artichoke hearts, drained
1	cup Parmesan cheese
1	cup mayonnaise
1	teaspoon onion flakes (to taste)
1	teaspoon chives

Preheat oven to 250 degrees.

Blend all ingredients thoroughly in a blender. Pour mixture into a 1-quart casserole dish. Bake for 45 minutes or until heated through and crust forms. Serve hot with fresh vegetables, bread sticks, or crackers.

Serves 8 to 10.

Mexican Artichoke Dip

This is a slightly different version of the artichoke dip with a Mexican twist.

1	can (8 1/2 ounce) artichoke hearts, drained and chopped
1	can (6 1/2 ounce) marinated artichoke hearts, drained and chopped
1	can (4 ounce) chopped green chilies, drained
2	cups shredded sharp Cheddar cheese
1	cup mayonnaise

Preheat oven at 350 degrees.

Combine artichokes in a 2-quart casserole dish. Sprinkle with chilies. Cover with cheese. Spoon teaspoons of mayonnaise on top until covered. Bake uncovered for 10 to 15 minutes or until cheese is melted. Serve with large tortilla chips.

Makes approximately 3 cups.

• •

Cold Shrimp and Cheese Dip

Quick and easy, but impressive!

---

1 1/2	**cups cleaned, cooked shrimp**
1	**tablespoon lemon juice**
1	**cup cream style cottage cheese**
5	**tablespoons chili sauce**
1	**teaspoon finely chopped onion**
1/2	**teaspoon Worchestershire sauce**
1	**cup milk**
2	**tablespoons sour cream**
1	**tablespoon finely chopped parsley**
1/2	**teaspoon salt**
1/8	**teaspoon pepper**

Finely chop shrimp. Combine with lemon juice, cottage cheese, chili sauce, onion, Worchestershire sauce, milk, sour cream, parsley, salt and pepper in a blender and blend until smooth.

Chill at least 30 minutes or until ready to serve. Serve with crackers.

Makes about 2 cups.

Crab Dip

You can use 1/2 pound of fresh crab meat instead of the canned,
if you have it. This is hard to resist!

---

1   **can (6 1/2 ounces) crabmeat, drained**
1   **cup mayonnaise**
1/2   **cup sour cream**
1   **tablespoon grated onion**
1   **tablespoon chopped parsley**
1/2   **teaspoon salt**
1   **tablespoon sherry**
1   **teaspoon lemon juice**
           dash of pepper

Remove any shell or cartilage from crabmeat. Combine crabmeat with mayonnaise, sour cream, onion, parsley, salt, sherry, lemon juice and pepper. Blend well.

Refrigerate several hours or overnight to let the flavors blend.

Makes about 2 cups.

Curry Dip

This tastes great with fresh vegetables.

2	**cups mayonnaise**
2	**teaspoons curry powder**
	juice from 2 lemons
1/2	**cup catsup**
1	**teaspoon chopped onion**
	dash of Tabasco sauce
	dash of Worchestershire sauce

Combine mayonnaise, curry powder, lemon juice, catsup, onion, Tabasco sauce and Worchestershire sauce. Blend well.

Chill for several hours before serving.

Makes approximately 3 cups.

Jalapeno Cheese Dip

If you like a spicy and cheesy dip - this one's for you!

1/2	**cup mayonnaise**
3/4	**cup sour cream**
1	**cup shredded Montery Jack cheese with jalapeno peppers**
2 1/2	**tablespoons chopped green onion**
1/2	**cup nuts**

Preheat oven to 350 degrees.

Combine mayonnaise, sour cream, cheese, onion, and nuts in a 1-quart casserole dish until blended. Bake for 15 minutes or until bubbling. Serve with tortilla chips.

Makes 3 cups.

Mexican Salsa

These two recipes are family treasures of the Franklin family.
Ralph Franklin, my son-in-law, is called on to make these often!

1	quart chopped (very ripe) fresh tomatoes or drained canned tomatoes
4 to 5	tablespoons chili powder to taste
3	cloves garlic, finely chopped
2	cans (5 ounces) chopped green chilies
3	medium onions, chopped
2	tablespoons coriander leaves (also called cilantro or Chinese parsley)
2 to 3	jalapenos, chopped, or more to taste
	salt and pepper to taste

Combine all ingredients in a large mixing bowl and blend well.

Cover and refrigerate a few hours before serving to blend flavors. Will keep up to 3 weeks in the refrigerator. Serve with tortilla chips.

Makes about 1 1/2 quarts.

Guacamole Dip

2	ripe avocados, peeled and finely chopped
	prepared Mexican salsa (see above)
	juice of 1 lime

Combine avocado with an equal amount of Mexican salsa. Add lime juice and blend well. Put 1 or 2 of the avocado pits into the dip to keep it from turning brown.

Cover and refrigerate before serving. Will keep up to 2 days in the refrigerator.

Remove pits and serve with tortilla chips.

Spinach Dip

When expecting guests, whip this up ahead of time - they'll love it!

1	package (10 ounces) frozen, chopped spinach, thawed
1 1/2	cups sour cream
1	cup mayonnaise
1	package Knorr Vegetable Soup Mix
1	can (8 ounces) water chestnuts, finely chopped
3	green onions, finely chopped

Squeeze spinach until dry. Combine spinach, sour cream, mayonnaise, soup mix, water chestnuts and onions in a mixing bowl.

Cover and refrigerate 2 hours. Serve with crackers or bread.

Makes 3 cups.

Vegetable Dip

This will keep several days.

1	pint sour cream
1	pint mayonnaise
3	tablespoons dill seed
1	tablespoon chopped onion
1 1/2	tablespoon seasoning salt
1	tablespoon dried parsley
1	tablespoon lemon juice

Combine sour cream, mayonnaise, dill seed, onion, salt, parsley, and lemon juice. Blend well.

Cover and refrigerate for 1 to 2 hours. Serve with fresh vegetables.

Makes approximately 3 cups.

Vidalia Onion Dip

Alice Wheatly of Beaufort (NC) shared this while sitting on her veranda overlooking the Beaufort waterway.

1   **cup chopped Vidalia or other sweet onions**
1   **cup Hellman's mayonnaise**
1   **cup grated sharp Cheddar cheese**

Preheat the oven to 350 degrees.

Butter a 1 1/2-quart baking dish. Combine all the ingredients in a medium size bowl and mix well. Transfer the ingredients to the prepared baking dish and bake for 20 minutes or until bubbly.

Serve with toast triangles or crackers.

Makes 8-10 servings.

Cream Puffs

These freeze well before you fill them. Crabmeat is my favorite filling, but they're also good with chicken or shrimp salad.

1/4	pound (1 stick) butter or margarine, softened
1	cup all-purpose flour
1/4	teaspoon salt
4	eggs

Preheat oven to 450 degrees.

Add butter to 1 cup of boiling water in a sauce pan. Stir until butter is melted. Add flour and salt (together). Cook on medium heat, stirring vigorously, until mixture is smooth and forms soft ball that does not separate.

Cool. Add eggs, one at a time, mixing well after each egg. Beat until smooth. Drop approximately 1 tablespoon of batter for each puff onto a greased cookie sheet. Bake for 15 minutes at 450 degrees, then reduce oven to 325 degrees and bake for 25 minutes. Cool and fill with your favorite filling.

Makes about 2 1/2 dozen.

Crabmeat Paste for Cream Puffs

1	pound crabmeat, drained
2	teaspoons horseradish
1/2	teaspoon prepared mustard
1	cup mayonnaise
1	teaspoon Worchestershire sauce
1	cup grated hard boiled egg
	salt to taste
	cream puffs

Remove bones from crabmeat and combine with horseradish, mustard, mayonnaise, Worchestershire sauce, egg and salt in a mixing bowl. Mix well. Spoon mixture into hollowed out cream puff shells. Garnish with grated egg or parsley.

Fills 30 puffs.

Deviled Ham Puffs

These are easy and real tasty, but be sure to serve while they're hot!

1	**package (8 ounces) cream cheese, softened**
1	**egg yolk, beaten**
1	**teaspoon onion juice**
1/2	**teaspoon baking powder**
	salt to taste
1/2	**teaspoon horseradish**
1/4	**teaspoon Tabasco sauce**
24	**small bread rounds**
1	**can (4 1/2 ounces) liverwurst spread or deviled ham**

Preheat oven to broil.

Blend together cheese, egg yolk, onion juice, baking powder, salt, horseradish and Tabasco sauce. Toast bread on one side. Remove from oven and reset oven to bake at 375 degrees.

Spread meat on untoasted side of bread. Cover each round with a mound of the cheese mixture. Place rounds on a cookie sheet. Bake for 10 or 12 minutes. Serve hot.

Makes 24 rounds.

Parmesan Puffs

If you like Parmesan cheese, you'll love this one!

3	ounces cream cheese
1	cup mayonnaise
1 1/2	teaspoon grated onion
1	cup grated Parmesan cheese plus additional for topping
1/4	teaspoon cayenne pepper
1	loaf thinly sliced bread
	paprika

Preheat oven to 300 degrees.

Mix cream cheese, mayonnaise, grated onion, Parmesan cheese and pepper. Cut bread into 2-inch rounds. Bake rounds on a cookie sheet for 15 to 20 minutes to dry out.

Spread cheese mixture generously on bread rounds. Sprinkle extra Parmesan cheese and paprika on top. Broil until puffy and golden brown. Serve hot.

Makes about 30.

Spinach Balls

An easy to make hors d'oeuvre that freezes well before cooking.
Polly Mayo from Kinston (NC) shared this with me.

2	**packages frozen chopped spinach (squeeze dry)**
2	**cups herb dressing**
1	**cup grated Parmesan cheese**
1	**stick butter or margarine, melted**
3	**eggs, slightly beaten**

Preheat oven to 375 degrees.

Combine spinach, herb dressing, cheese, butter and eggs in a mixing bowl. Form into balls, approximately 1 inch in diameter. Place balls on a greased cookie sheet and bake for 10 or 15 minutes.

Makes about 50 balls.

Turnovers

This recipe and the mushroom filling came from Kitty Bailey of New Bern.

1	**package (8 ounces) cream cheese, softened**
1/2	**pound (2 sticks) butter or margarine, softened**
	dash of salt
2	**cups sifted all-purpose flour**
1	**egg yolk**
2	**teaspoons cream or milk**

Combine cheese, butter and salt. Work in the flour with a fork or your fingers until a smooth dough is formed. Refrigerate for several hours or overnight before using. Roll dough on a floured surface to about 1/8 inch thickness and cut into 3-inch round circles.

Place a teaspoon of filling just off center of each circle. Fold dough over filling and crimp edges with a floured fork. Freeze turnovers uncovered on a tray. Place frozen turnovers in a plastic bag for freezer storage. When ready to serve, brush tops with beaten egg yolk and cream. Bake frozen turnovers in 375 degree oven for 15 to 20 minutes.

Makes 40 turnovers.

Mushroom Filling for Turnover

1/2	**pound fresh mushrooms**
3	**tablespoons butter or margarine**
1	**small onion, minced**
2	**teaspoons all-purpose flour**
	salt and pepper to taste
1/2	**cup sour cream**
1	**teaspoon dried dill**

Wash mushrooms, then trim off toughest stems and chop finely. Melt butter in a skillet, then saute onions and mushrooms until tender. Add flour, salt and pepper. Cook for 1 to 2 minutes. Remove from heat and stir in sour cream and dill.

Cool and fill pastry.

Cocktail Weiners

Guests, especially the men, love these.

1	**pound all beef weiners**
1/2	**cup brown sugar**
1/2	**cup vinegar**
1/2	**cup bourbon**
1/2	**cup catsup**

Cut weiners into bite size pieces. Combine sugar, vinegar, bourbon, and catsup in a sauce pan. Simmer weiners in sauce for about 1 hour.

Pour into a chafing dish and use immediately or refrigerate and heat to serve at a later time.

Serves 6 to 8.

Fried Eggplant

Select a good, firm eggplant for the best results.

---

1   **eggplant**
        oil for frying

Beer batter:
1   **can (12 ounces) beer**
1 1/2   **cups self-rising flour**

Peel and cut the eggplant in strips about 3 inches long and 1/2-inch thick. Cover with water and soak until ready to serve to keep from turning brown.

Drain eggplant thoroughly and pat dry. Prepare beer batter by combining beer and flour. Mix together well and then let stand a few minutes before using.

Heat oil over high heat. Dip eggplant into the batter and fry in deep fat until brown and crispy. Drain on paper towels and sprinkle with salt.

Makes enough for 4 to 6 people.

Hot Sausage Balls I

These are different, but equally delicious. You can freeze the sausage balls in the second recipe for later use.

2   pounds hot pork sausage
1   small jar Major Grey's chutney, finely chopped
     sherry (fill chutney jar to measure)
1   cup sour cream

Roll sausage into bit-size meat balls. Fry slowly in a skillet until well done. Pour off grease and transfer balls to a chafing dish. Combine chutney, sherry and sour cream in a skillet. Cook gently until heated. Pour over sausage.

Makes enough for 12 to 15 people as an hors d'oeuvre.

Hot Sausage Balls II

1   pound hot pork sausage
12   ounces sharp Cheddar cheese, grated
3   cups Bisquick
     dash of red pepper

Preheat oven to 350 degrees.

Mix all ingredients together thoroughly. Shape into balls about the size of a marble. Bake for 20 minutes or until golden. Do not overcook.

Makes about 24.

Sweet and Pungent Meatballs

These are almost a must for cocktail parties.

Meatballs:

1 1/2	pounds ground pork	1	tablespoon sherry
1	small onion, minced	2	tablespoons soy sauce
1/2	cup chopped fresh mushrooms	2	tablespoons cornstarch
		1	teaspoon sugar
1/2	teaspoon salt dash of pepper		peanut oil for frying

Sauce:

1	can (9 ounces) pineapple chunks, drain and save syrup	2	tablespoons vinegar
		2	carrots, thinly sliced
		2	green peppers, seeded and cut into slices
1 1/2	tablespoons oil		
1	tablespoon brown sugar	1	tomato, peeled and cut into wedges
1/2	teaspoon salt	1	tablespoon cornstarch

Mix pork with onion, mushroom, salt, pepper, sherry, soy sauce, cornstarch and sugar in a mixing bowl. Shape sausage mixture into balls about the size of an apricot. Fry in heated oil until meatballs are brown on the outside and cooked inside. Drain on a paper towel.

Heat pineapple syrup with oil, brown sugar, salt and vinegar until bubbling. Add carrots and green pepper and cook 1 minute. Add tomato, pineapple and meatballs and cook until sauce bubbles no longer. Mix cornstarch with 1/4 cup cold water until a smooth paste is formed and stir into meatball mixture. Cook until slightly thick. This may be prepared ahead of time and reheated at serving time.

Serves 8 to 10.

Stuffed Mushrooms I

Mushrooms and crabmeat are a great combination. The sherry makes them extra special.

18	medium to large mushrooms
5	tablespoons butter or margarine
1	small onion, minced
1 1/2	tablespoons all-purpose flour
3/4	cup white crabmeat
2	tablespoons sherry
1 1/2	tablespoons chopped parsley
	salt and pepper to taste
1/4	cup cornflake crumbs

Preheat oven to 350 degrees.

Trim stems from mushrooms and place cap side down on greased cookie sheet. Chop stems. Melt 4 tablespoons of butter in a skillet and saute onions. Add mushroom stems. Cook 5 minutes. Stir in flour and blend well. Add crabmeat, sherry, parsley, salt and pepper.

Stuff mushroom caps with crabmeat filling and sprinkle cornflake crumbs on top of each mushroom. Dot with remaining butter. Bake for 15 minutes or until heated through. These can be prepared ahead of time and heated just prior to serving.

Makes 18 servings.

Stuffed Mushrooms II

If you can't get crabmeat, this sausage stuffing is almost as good.

12	large mushrooms
1	pound pork sausage
1	onion, minced
1/3	cup canned bread crumbs
1/4	teaspoon sage
2	tablespoons sherry
1/8	teaspoon salt

Trim stems from mushrooms and place cap side down on greased cookie sheet. Chop stems. Cook sausage in a skillet until done. Add chopped mushroom stems and onion. Cook for 2 minutes more. Drain excess fat from skillet, then add bread crumbs, sage, sherry and salt.

Stuff mushroom caps with sausage filling. Broil until heated through. These can be prepared ahead of time and heated just prior to serving.

Makes 12 servings.

Pickled Mushrooms

Be sure to prepare ahead!

3	medium onions
3/4	cup vinegar
1/2	teaspoon leaf marjoram
1/4	teaspoon whole cloves
1/2	teaspoon celery seed
1/2	teaspoon mustard seed
1	tablespoon salt
1/4	teaspoon hot sauce
1/2	pound fresh mushrooms, washed
1/4	cup olive oil

Cut onions into 1/2 inch slices, separate, and cook in 3/4 cup of water, vinegar and spices for 5 minutes. Add mushrooms and cook 5 more minutes. Remove mushrooms and add olive oil to onions and liquid. Bring to a boil and pour over mushrooms. Let stand 3 hours or longer. Can be used as an hors d'oeuvre or a salad.

Serves 4.

Easy Marinated Shrimp

This is a quick and easy hors d'oeuvre from Alice Wheatly of Beaufort (NC).

1	stick butter or margarine
3	pounds peeled, uncooked shrimp
	salt to taste
	garlic salt to taste
1	bottle (16 ounces) Italian dressing
1	red onion, sliced
1	green pepper, seeded and sliced
1	cucumber, peeled and sliced

Melt the butter in a large skillet and saute shrimp until pink. Sprinkle with salt and garlic salt. Cool. Place shrimp in a marinade container or a container with a top that fits tightly. Pour in dressing and stir well. Refrigerate overnight, stirring occasionally.

When ready to serve, garnish with red onion, pepper, and cucumber.

Serves approximately 20.

Pickled Shrimp

Laura Weyher, my good friend from New York, taught me this one! Give yourself at least 2 days prep time.

3	pounds shrimp, shelled and deveined
2	cups vinegar
1	cup lemon juice
1	cup salad oil
2	tablespoons sugar
6	bay leaves
1	teaspoon crushed black pepper
	dash of Worchestershire sauce
1	teaspoon dill seed
1/2	teaspoon dried tarragon leaves
1	teaspoon celery salt
1	teaspoon dry mustard
1	teaspoon salt
3	medium onions, thinly sliced
	chopped parsley

Bring 6 cups of water to a boil in a large saucepan. Add shrimp. Bring to a boil again and cook for about 3 minutes. Drain shrimp and set aside.

In same saucepan, combine vinegar, lemon juice, oil, sugar, bay leaves, pepper, Worchestershire sauce, dill seed, tarragon leaves, celery salt, mustard and salt. Bring to a boil. Cook for 10 minutes.

Place a layer of shrimp in a large shallow dish. Cover with onion rings. Repeat with remaining shrimp and onions. Pour on hot marinade. Let stand until cool. Cover and refrigerate. Stir occasionally over the next 2 days before serving.

To serve, drain shrimp and onions. Arrange on a platter. Sprinkle with parsley.

Serves 10 to 12 as an hors d'oeuvres.

Hot Pepper Jelly

This is wonderful spread over cream cheese and served with crackers.

1	**cup (about 2 large peppers) seeded and finely chopped green pepper**
1/4	**cup crushed red pepper**
1 1/2	**cups vinegar**
6 1/2	**cups sugar**
	green or red food coloring
1	**bottle (6 ounces) liquid fruit pectin**
4	**jelly jars (4 ounces)**
	melted paraffin

Place 1/2 cup of vinegar in a blender and add green peppers and red pepper. Blend until pureed. Strain pepper mixture through a fine cheese cloth, squeezing hard. Pour juice into a large saucepan and add remaining vinegar, sugar, and food coloring. Bring mixture to a full rolling boil for about 10 minutes, stirring constantly. Remove from heat and cool 5 minutes.

Skim off thick foam that rises to the top. Add liquid pectin and stir well. Pour into hot sterilized glasses. Cover jelly with melted paraffin, 1/8 inch thick.

Makes 4 jars.

8 Day Cucumber Pickles

Forty years ago, my mother, Helen Jones, from Greenville (NC) made and sold these at her country home.

2	**cups salt**
2	**gallons whole cucumbers, washed**
2	**packages powdered alum**
8	**cups sugar**
2	**tablespoons celery seed**
1/4	**cup pickling spices**
2	**quarts vinegar**
5	**sticks cinnamon**

Place cucumbers in a very large stockpot. Dissolve salt in one gallon of water. Boil and pour over cucumbers. Cover and leave 1 week.

Pour off brine and rinse well. Cover with boiling water and let stand, covered, for 24 hours, then drain. Boil one gallon water and add alum. Pour over cucumbers. Let stand, covered, for 24 hours and then drain. Cut pickles as desired.

Mix sugar, celery seed, spices, vinegar and cinnamon sticks in a large saucepan. Heat to boiling. Pour over cucumbers. Cover and let cool. Heat to boil each morning for 2 more days.

Pack into sterilized glasses and seal while hot.

Makes 12 pints.

One Day Cucumber Pickles

This quick pickle recipe was shared by Carolyn Holding, from Raleigh (NC).

12	medium-sized cucumbers, cut into 1/4 inch slices
1 1/2	pounds onions, thinly sliced
1/2	cup salt
3	cups vinegar
3	cups sugar
1/2	teaspoon tumeric
1/4	cup mustard seed
2	teaspoons celery seed
1/4	teaspoon cayenne pepper

Combine cucumbers in a glass or stainlees steel bowl with onions and salt. Let the mixture stand for 3 hours, then pour into a colander to drain. Rinse with cold water and drain again. Rinse and drain again.

Combine vinegar, sugar, and spices in a large saucepan. Bring to a boil, then add drained cucumber mixture. Bring just to a simmer and cook for 2 minutes (avoid boiling - it would soften the cucumber slices). Cool the pickles you want to serve immediately, then place in a covered bowl and refrigerate. Pack the remaining pickles in hot, sterilized jars.

Makes 4 to 5 pints.

Green Tomato Pickles

This is another of my mother's great pickle recipes. She always did make the best!

3	**cups lime**
7	**pounds green tomatoes**
4 1/2	**pounds sugar**
3	**pints vinegar**
1	**teaspoon ground cloves**
1	**teaspoon ginger**
1	**teaspoon allspice**
1	**teaspoon celery seed**
1	**teaspoon mace**
1	**teaspoon cinnamon**

Dissolve lime in two gallons of water. Add tomatoes and soak for 24 hours. Drain thoroughly and soak in fresh water for 4 hours, draining and replacing water every hour. Drain and pat dry.

Place sugar, vinegar, and spices in a saucepan. All the tomatoes and bring to a boil. Remove from heat. Cover and let stand overnight. Boil for one hour, then seal in hot, sterilized jars. Be careful when handling the tomatoes because they will break easily.

Makes 10 pints.

Watermelon Rind Pickles

Doris Wessell from Leland (NC) shared this one that is just like mother made. Lilley's lime can be found at your local pharmacy.

8	pounds watermelon rind, peeled and cut into small shapes
1	tube Lilley's lime
7	pounds sugar
1 1/2	quarts white vinegar
1/4	package (.6 ounces) whole cloves
1/4	package (.75 ounces) stick cinnamon

Place rinds in a very large stockpot. Dissolve lime in enough cold water to cover the rind. Cover and let rind soak in the lime overnight. Drain and rinse the rind the next morning.

Place the stockpot with the rind on the stove. Fill with cold water to cover the rind. Bring to a boil. Drain and cool. Fill with cold water again and boil for 1 hour. Drain well.

Combine the sugar, vinegar, and spices in a large stockpot over medium heat. Let the syrup come to a boil. Drop in the rind and cook until the rind becomes slightly transparent.

Place the pickles in sterilized jars with enough syrup to cover the rind.

Makes 10 pints.

Beverages

Beverages ●

Coffee Punch

Chocolate ice cream is also good with this.

1	**gallon strong coffee**
10	**tablespoons sugar**
1 1/2	**teaspoon almond flavoring**
1	**quart heavy cream, whipped**
1	**quart vanilla ice cream, broken into spoonfuls**

While coffee is still hot, sweeten with sugar. Cool coffee in the refrigerator until cold. Just before serving, add almond flavoring, cream, and ice cream. Mix well.

Makes about 60 punch cups.

Hot Cranberry-Apple Drink

This tastes great after skiing, chopping wood, or any exercise outside on a cold day!

1 1/2	quarts cranberry juice
2	quarts apple juice
	juice from 1 lemon
	grated rind from 1 lemon
4	sticks cinnamon
1/2	cup brown sugar
1/2	teaspoon salt
1 1/2	teaspoons whole cloves

Combine cranberry juice, apple juice, lemon juice, and lemon rind in a large soup pot and bring to a boil. Add cinnamon, sugar, salt and cloves. Boil gently for 10 minutes. Strain and serve. This keeps well in the refrigerator.

Serves 20.

Instant Hot Chocolate

Prepare ahead for the cold days of winter.

1   box (8 quarts) instant milk
1   box (1 pound) Hersey's Instant Cocoa Mix
3/4   box confectioner's sugar
        pinch of salt

Mix milk, cocoa mix, sugar and salt well. Use 1/2 cup of mix per cup of hot water.

Instant Spiced Tea

1   jar (1 pound, 2 ounces) Tang
3/4   cup instant tea
1 1/2   cups sugar
2   envelopes powdered instant sweetened lemonade
1   teaspoon ground cloves
1/2   teaspoon cinnamon
1/2   teaspoon allspice

Mix Tang, tea, sugar, lemonade, cloves, cinnamon, and allspice well. Store in a tight container. To serve, use 3 teaspoons of mixture per cup of boiling water.

Bloody Mary Mix

Keeps well in the refrigerator for a week.

2 1/2	cups tomato juice
1 1/2	teaspoon Worchestershire sauce
1	teaspoon horseradish
1	teaspoon celery salt
	ground pepper
	juice from 3 lemons
6	stalks celery
	vodka to taste

Combine tomato juice, Worchestershire sauce, horseradish, celery salt, pepper, and lemon juice. Chill. Stir in vodka just before serving. Serve over ice and garnish with celery.

Serves 6.

Cider Punch

This punch is good for wedding receptions or showers.

1	**gallon apple cider**
1	**quart pineapple juice**
3	**quarts orange juice**
1	**quart lemonade**
3	**quarts ginger ale or lemon-lime carbonated drink**
6	**bottles champagne**

Chill juices until icy cold. Combine cider, pineapple juice, orange juice, lemonade, and ginger ale in a large punch bowl. Add champagne.

Makes 50 cups or approximately 3 gallons.

Egg Nog

This is very rich and very good... a favorite of our family on Christmas morning.

12	eggs, separated
1	cup sugar
1	quart milk or half and half
2	cups bourbon
1	cup rum
1	quart heavy cream, whipped

Beat egg yolks until very thick. Add sugar slowly, beating continuously. Add bourbon and rum gradually. Add milk. Fold in whipped cream. Beat egg whites until stiff, then fold into the milk mixture.

Makes about 4 quarts.

Irish Coffee

For the coffee lover... for dessert or just for relaxing.

1	**teaspoon instant coffee**
1	**teaspoon sugar**
1/4	**shot glass Irish whiskey**
	whipped cream or ice cream for topping

Combine coffee and 4 ounces of boiling water. Add sugar and whiskey, then stir. Top with cream.

Makes 1 serving.

Whiskey Sour Punch

This is good for any kind of party.

2	cans (12 ounces each) frozen orange juice
1	can (12 ounces) frozen lemonade
3	liters ginger ale
1	liter club soda
1	fifth bourbon whiskey

Combine orange juice and lemonade with ginger ale and club soda. Add bourbon just before serving. Serve over ice.

Serves approximately 10 to 15 (1 punchbowl).

_____

_____

_____

_____

_____

_____

_____

_____

_____

_____

Beverages ●

_____

_____

_____

_____

_____

_____

_____

_____

_____

Soups

Soups •

Broccoli Cheese Soup

A broccoli lover's delight!

4	cups chicken stock
1	large bunch broccoli, cleaned and cup into 1-inch pieces
1	large onion, sliced
6	ounces sharp Cheddar cheese, grated
1	cup sour cream
	salt and pepper to taste
2	tablespoons butter or margarine
	croutons

Place chicken stock in a stock pot and bring to a boil. Add the broccoli and onion and cook over medium heat until vegetables are tender.

Place a portion of the vegetables and stock plus half the cheese in a blender and puree until smooth and no lumps remain. Repeat the process until all stock, vegetables and cheese have been pureed. Add salt and pepper (if canned stock was used, do not add additional salt). Stir in sour cream. Add butter and reheat complete mixture.

Top with a few croutons prior to serving.

Serves 4 to 6.

Clam Chowder

This is a versatile recipe for either Manhattan or New England chowder that can be prepared ahead and frozen until ready to use.

1	pint fresh (or fresh frozen) chowder clams
4	medium potatoes, cubed
1	large onion, chopped fine
8	slices bacon, fried crisp and crumbled, reserve grease
	salt and pepper to taste
2	tablespoons Worchestershire sauce

For Manhattan chowder:

1	can (16 ounces) whole tomatoes, chopped
1/2	teaspoon hot pepper sauce

OR

For New England chowder:

1	quart half and half (light cream)

Drain clams, reserving juice. Chop clams. Combine clams, clam juice, 4 cups of water, potatoes, onions, bacon, bacon grease, salt, pepper, and Worchestershire sauce in a 3-quart soup pot. Cook over medium heat, stirring occasionally, until potatoes are tender. At this point you can freeze the soup mixture for later use or continue to prepare.

For the red, Manhattan chowder, add the tomatoes and hot sauce. For the white, New England chowder, add the half and half. Heat before serving.

Serves 8.

Down East Clam Chowder

This is the preferred version "down east" (on the coast) in North
Carolina and Kate Salter from Beaufort makes the best!

4	slices streak of lean salt pork
1	quart chowder clams, chopped (do not grind)
	salt and pepper to taste
2	medium onions, chopped
4	medium potatoes, cut into small cubes
	corn meal dumplings

Corn meal dumplings:

1	cup plain corn meal
1/3	cup all-purpose flour
	dash of salt

Fry streak of lean pork in a skillet. Add 2 quarts of water. Bring to a boil. Add clams, salt and pepper. Cook slowly for 2 hours or until clams are tender. Add additional hot water, if needed.

Add potatoes and onions and cook until potatoes are done.

While poatoes are cooking, prepare the dumplings. Combine corn meal, flour, and salt with enough water to form small balls. Pat each ball flat and drop into chowder. Cover and simmer about 15 to 20 minutes. Remove pork slices before serving.

Serves 12 to 14.

Crab Bisque

This recipe came from Amine Edwards, my sister-in-law from Rocky Mount (NC).

1	can green pea soup, undiluted
1	can tomato soup, undiluted
1	can consome
1	can mushroom soup, undiluted
1	cup half and half
1	pound fresh crabmeat, drained
	sherry to taste

Place soups in a blender. Blend well. Add half and half, crabmeat and sherry. Blend until smooth. Place in a saucepan and let simmer for 15 minutes. Serve hot or cold.

Serves 8.

Gazpacho

This tastes great for lunch on a hot summer day.

4	cups peeled and diced tomatoes
1 1/2	cups chopped green pepper
3/4	cup chopped green onion
1/4	teaspoon garlic salt
2	cups beef boullion
1/2	cup lemon juice
1/4	cup olive oil
1	tablespoon paprika
1	tablespoon salt
	fresh ground pepper to taste
1/2	cup diced cucumbers

Combine tomatoes, green pepper, onion, garlic salt, boullion, lemon juice, olive oil, paprika, salt and pepper. Let stand at room temperature for 1 hour, stirring frequently.

Chill at least 2 hours before serving. Add cucumbers just before serving.

Makes 6 servings.

Fresh Mushroom Soup

You'll never used canned again!

3	**tablespoons vegetable oil**
1 1/2	**cups (2 medium) chopped white onions**
1	**cup chopped green onion**
1/4	**cup uncooked converted long-grain white rice**
4	**cups (1 12-ounce package) sliced fresh mushrooms**
6	**cups canned or homemade chicken broth**
1/2	**teaspoon salt**
1/8	**teaspoon ground pepper**

Heat oil in a 3 quart saucepan over moderate heat. Add onions and cook for 3 to 4 minutes, stirring frequently until soft and clear. Add rice and mushrooms and cook 2 minutes longer, stirring frequently. Add broth, 2 cups of water, salt and pepper. Cover and simmer for 20 minutes or until rice is tender.

Remove from heat and put one cup of mixture in a blender. Cover and blend 40 seconds at low speed until pureed. Pour into a large bowl and repeat with remaining mixture. Pour pureed mixture back into the saucepan and heat over low temperature until hot.

Makes ten (1 cup) servings.

French Onion Soup

You'll get raves from this.

4   **medium onions, very thinly sliced**
2   **tablespoons butter or margarine, melted**
4   **cups beef broth**
1   **teaspoon thyme**
      salt and pepper to taste
1/2   **cup sherry**
      Parmesan croutons (see recipe below)
1/2   **cup shredded Swiss cheese**

Preheat oven to 400 degrees.

Cook onions in butter in a large, covered skillet until onions are tender, about 5 minutes. Uncover skillet and continue cooking until onions are well browned, stiring occasionally. Stir in broth, 1/2 cup of water and thyme. Cover and simmer for 30 minutes. Add salt, pepper and wine. Ladle soup into individual ovenproof dishes. Place a Parmesan crouton on each serving and sprinkle with Swiss cheese. Bake for 15 minutes or until cheese is melted and golden brown.

Makes 4 to 6 servings.

Parmesan Croutons

2 to 3   **slices (1 inch thick) French bread, cut in half**
1/4   **cup butter or margarine, melted**
1/4   **cup grated Parmesan cheese**

Preheat oven to 350 degrees.

Brush both sides of bread with butter. Sprinkle with Parmesan cheese. Place on a cookie sheet and bake for 20 minutes or until crisp and brown.

Makes 4 to 6 large croutons.

Peanut Soup

You'd think you were in Virginia!

1/4	cup butter
3/4	cup diced celery
3/4	cup diced onion
6	cups chicken stock or broth
4	teaspoons all-purpose flour
3/4	cup creamy peanut butter
1	cup cream (optional)
6	tablespoons chopped, salted peanuts for garnish

Melt butter in saucepan over low heat. Add celery and onions. Cook until tender but not brown. Stir in chicken broth. Bring to boil for one minute. Strain. Return to saucepan. Cool to room temperature.

Mix flour with just enough cool water to form paste. Stir into broth. Blend in peanut butter. Simmer slowly 15 minutes, stirring occasionally. Add a cup of cream, if desired, just before removing soup from heat.

Serve hot. Garnish each serving with a tablespoon of chopped, salted peanuts.

Makes 6 servings.

Shrimp Soup

A spicy shrimp delight.

12	ounces tomato soup
4	cups chicken stock or broth
1/3	cup dry white wine
1/2	cup peeled and diced tomatoes
1/3	cup chopped onion
1/2	cup chopped celery
1/4	teaspoon coarse ground black pepper
1 1/2	teaspoons minced garlic
1	teaspoon sweet basil
1/4	teaspoon tarragon
1/8	teaspoon paprika
1	bay leaf
5 to 10 drops hot pepper sauce to taste	
1	pound small raw shrimp, cleaned

Combine tomato soup, broth, wine, tomatoes, onion, celery, pepper, garlic, basil, tarragon, paprika, bay leaf, and hot pepper sauce in a soup pot and bring to a boil. Reduce heat and simmer 10 minutes. Add shrimp 5 minutes before serving. As soon as shrimp are pink and firm, the soup is ready.

Serve with French bread or crackers.

Makes 6 servings.

Shrimp and Corn Chowder

This was a favorite of Laura Wallace, a good friend from Morehead City.

1/2	**pound bacon, fried crisp (reserve 3 tablespoons bacon grease)**
2	**cups minced onions**
1	**cup finely chopped celery**
1/2	**cup finely chopped green pepper**
1/2	**cup grated carrots**
1/2	**bay leaf, crumpled**
2	**cups diced potatoes**
2	**tablespoons all-purpose flour**
2	**pounds shrimp, cooked and peeled (reserve 4 cups shrimp stock)**
1	**can (16 1/2 ounces) cream style corn**
1	**can (16 1/2 ounces) whole corn**
1	**can (13 ounces) evaporated milk**
1	**teaspoon salt**
1/2	**teaspoon black pepper**
1/2	**teaspoon cayenne pepper**
	tabasco to taste

Crumble bacon and set aside. Reserve bacon grease. Saute onion, celery, bell pepper and carrots in bacon grease. Add bay leaf, potatoes and 1/4 cup of water. Cook for 5 to 10 minutes. Sprinkle flour over mixture, stir well and add shrimp stock. Bring to a boil. Add shrimp, corn, milk, salt, pepper and tabasco. Simmer over low heat for approximately 30 minutes.

Sprinkle bacon on top to garnish.

Makes 8 servings.

Salads

Salads ●●●●●●●●●●●●●●●●●●●●●●●●●●●●●●●●●●

Apple Cider Salad

This is a favorite over the Christmas holidays.

2	packages (3 ounces each) lemon gelatin
2	cups hot apple cider or juice
2	cups cold apple cider
4	teaspoons lemon juice
1/2	teaspoon salt
2	cups diced apples
1	cup seeded grape halves
1/2	cup chopped olives

Dissolve gelatin in hot cider. Add cold cider, lemon juice, and salt. Chill until partially set. Stir in apples, grapes, and olives. Pour into individual molds and chill for 4 hours or until firm.

Serves 6 to 8.

Apricot-Orange Salad

This makes a pretty fall salad.

2	**packages (3 ounces each) orange Jello**
2	**cups apricot nectar**
1	**cup mandarin oranges, drained**
2	**bananas, sliced**
1	**cup miniature marshmallows**
1	**cup whipped cream or Dream Whip**

Dissolve Jello in 1 cup of hot water. Stir nectar in and chill until syrupy. Add oranges, bananas, marshmallows, and whipped cream. Pour into a 1 1/2 quart mold. Chill.

Serves 6 to 8.

Asparagus Mold I

Either of these are great for your next luncheon.

---

1   **package (3 ounces) lime Jello**
1   **tablespoon sweet pickle juice**
1/2   **teaspoon salt**
1   **cup mayonnaise**
1/2   **cup milk**
1/2   **cup grated Cheddar cheese**
1   **cup green asparagus, cut into small pieces**
1   **tablespoon onion juice**
     red pepper to taste

Dissolve Jello in 1 cup boiling water. Add 1/3 cup cold water, vinegar, salt, mayonnaise, milk, cheese, asparagus, onion juice, and red pepper. Pour into individual molds and chill for 4 hours or until firm.

Serves 6.

Asparagus Mold II

1   **package (4 ounces) cream cheese**
1   **package (3 ounces) lemon Jello**
1/2   **cup mayonnaise**
1   **can (15 ounces) green asparagus**
1/4   **cup slivered almonds, toasted**

Drain asparagus, reserving juice. Mash well.

Whip juice and cream cheese together. Add well mashed asparagus and mayonnaise. Dissolve gelatin in 1 cup boiling water. When cool, add to asparagus mixture. Add almonds. Place in a medium ring mold or 8 small individual molds. Chill for 4 hours or until firm.

Serves 8.

Asparagus Mold III

*My kids love asparagus, so I've found several ways to use them.
So, here's another one that's great for a luncheon.*

3/4	cup sugar
1/2	cup vinegar
1	tablespoon lemon juice
1/2	teaspoon salt
1	envelope (1 tablespoon) unflavored gelatin
1	cup chopped celery
1/2	cup chopped pecans
2	whole pimentos, chopped
1	can (10 1/2 ounces) cut asparagus, drained
2	teaspoons grated onion
1/2	cup stuffed olives, chopped
	mayonnaise

Combine sugar, vinegar, lemon juice, 1 cup water, and salt in a saucepan and bring to a boil. Boil for 2 minutes. Soften gelatin in 1/2 cup cold water. Add vinegar mixture, stirring until dissolved. Chill until syrupy. Fold in remaining ingredients except mayonnaise. Spoon mixture into 1 1/2 quart mold and chill until firm.

Serve with mayonnaise.

Serves 6 to 8.

Congealed Beet Salad

This was a favorite of my mother-in-law, Amine Galbreath, from Kinston (NC).

1	package (3 ounces) lemon Jello
1	envelope plain gelatin
1	cup canned pickled beets, chopped
3/4	cup pickled beet juice
1/2	teaspoon salt
2	teaspoons grated onion
1	tablespoon horseradish
3/4	cup diced celery
3	tablespoons vinegar

Dissolve Jello and gelatin in 1 cup of hot water. Add beets, beet juice, salt, onion, horseradish, celery and vinegar. Pour into individual molds. Chill for 4 hours or until firm.

Serves 6.

Broccoli Salad

Helen Blair, my friend from Morehead City (NC), used to say that this is even better the second day.

1	**bunch broccoli**
1	**medium onion, chopped**
3	**hard boiled eggs, chopped**
1/2	**cup spanish olives, chopped**
	mayonnaise
	lettuce

Finely chop the buds of the broccoli and just a little of the stalk. Combine broccoli, onions, eggs, and olives with just enough mayonnaise to hold the ingredients together. Refrigerate and serve when ready. Serve on a lettuce leaf.

Serves 4 to 6.

Cabbage Salad

This is great with seafood. Will keep up to 3 weeks in the refrigerator.

1	large cabbage, cored and shredded
1	medium green pepper, seeded and chopped
6 to 8	stuffed olives, sliced
1	large onion, chopped
1	carrot, chopped

Dressing:

1/2	cup olive oil
1	cup vinegar
1	tablespoon salt
1/2	cup sugar
1	teaspoon celery seed
1/2	teaspoon dry mustard

Combine cabbage, green pepper, olives, onion, and carrot in a large bowl. Combine oil, vinegar, salt, sugar, celery seed, and mustard in a separate bowl and stir until well blended. Pour dressing over slaw and tightly cover.

Serves 4 to 6.

Hot Slaw

This variation on the traditional slaw recipe is a favorite of Millie Thomas' from Burlington and Beaufort (NC).

1	**medium to large head of cabbage**
1	**heaping tablespoon Crisco**
1	**teaspoon salt**
1	**tablespoon sugar**
	pepper to taste
1/2	**pint heavy cream**
2	**tablespoon vinegar**

Cut cabbage in thin slices. Melt Crisco in a large, heavy pot. add the cabbage. Cover and cook on low heat until the cabbage is soft, but still slightly firm. Stir often.

Add salt, sugar and pepper. Mix well. Pour in cream. If more broth is desired, add some milk or half and half. Add vinegar and stir well. Serve hot or as soon as possible.

Serves 8.

Caesar Salad

This is a quick and easy version of Caesar salad. Garnish with anchovy fillets, if desired.

1/2	cup olive or salad oil
1	large clove garlic, minced very finely
1/4	teaspoon dry mustard
1	egg, beaten
1	tablespoon Worchestershire sauce
1/4	cup lemon juice
1/2	teaspoon salt
1/2	cup grated Parmesan cheese
1	head Romaine lettuce, cleaned and torn
	freshly ground pepper
1	cup croutons

Combine garlic, oil, mustard, egg, Worchestershire sauce, lemon juice, salt, pepper, and cheese in a jar and shake well. Pour over the lettuce. Grind pepper to taste over the lettuce. Add croutons and toss well.

Serves 4.

Cherry and Cream Cheese Salad

This recipe came from a great cook and a special friend,
Carolane Langley of Kinston (NC).

1	large can (20 ounces) crushed pinapple
1	can (15 ounces) Queen Anne cherries
1	large package cherry gelatin
1	package (8 ounces) cream cheese
1	bottle (16 ounces) cola
1/2	cup chopped nuts
	lettuce
	mayonnaise

Drain cherries and pineapple, reserving juices. Heat juices to boiling. Remove from heat and add gelatin. Stir until dissolved. Add cream cheese and cola. Mix well. Pour into an oiled 6-cup mold and chill until partially set.

Fold in cherries, pineapple and nuts. Chill until firm. Unmold onto lettuce and garnish with mayonnaise.

Serves 6 to 8.

Sour Cherry Salad

If you like tart ... you'll love this.

1	can (1 pound) red, sour cherries
1	can (1 pound, 4 1/2 ounces) crushed pineapple
1/2	cup sugar
1	orange
1	lemon
1	envelope unflavored gelatin
1	package (3 ounces) cherry gelatin
	lettuce
	sour cream

Drain cherries and pineapple, reserving liquid. Pour sugar over cherries. Grate orange and lemon rind, then squeeze the juices. Combine orange and lemon juice with enough reserved liquid from the cherries and pineapple plus water to make 2 1/2 cups of liquid.

Soften unflavored gelatin in 1/2 cup cold water. Heat 1 cup of the combined juices to boiling. Remove from heat and add cherry gelatin and softened unflavored gelatin. Stir until dissolved. Add remaining juice mixture and stir. Add cherries, pineapple, and grated rind. Pour into an oiled 6-cup mold or 8 individual molds.

Chill until firm. Unmold onto lettuce. Serve with sour cream.

Serves 8.

Sweet Cherry Salad

I make this during the Christmas holidays - it's a special treat and fits right in with your Christmas decor!

2	**cans (16 ounces each) pitted, dark sweet cherries**
1	**package (6 ounces) cherry gelatin**
3/4	**cup port wine**
2/3	**cup chopped pecans**
	lettuce
	mayonnaise

Drain cherries, reserving liquid. Cut cherries in half and set aside. Add enough water to liquid to make 2 1/2 cups. Bring liquid to a boil. Remove from heat and add gelatin. Stir until gelatin dissolves. Add wine. Chill until partially set. Fold in cherries and pecans. Spoon mixture into an oiled, 6-cup mold or 8 individual molds.

Cover and chill until firm. Unmold onto lettuce and serve with mayonnaise.

Serves 8.

Fancy Chicken Salad

Serve over lettuce or in patty shells for a luncheon or in miniature patty shells for an hors d'oeuvre.

2	cups cooked chicken, cut into bite-sized chunks
1/4	cup sliced water chestnuts
1/2	pound seedless green grapes, cut in half
1/2	cup chopped celery
1/2	cup slivered almonds, toasted
11	can (8 ounces) pineapple chunks, drained
3/4	cup mayonnaise
1	teapsoon curry powder
2	teaspoons soy sauce
2	teaspoons lemon juice

Combine chicken, water chestnuts, grapes, celery, almonds, pineapple, mayonnaise, curry powder, soy sauce, and lemon juice in a large mixing bowl. Mix well. Cover and chill for several hours.

Serves 6 to 8.

Old fashioned Chicken Salad

My family likes this with lots of red pepper and lemon juice. It's a winner. Great for sandwiches, too!

---

2   cups cooked chicken, cut into bite-sized pieces
1   cup chopped celery
1/4   teaspoon red pepper or to taste
2   tablespoons lemon juice or to taste
        salt to taste
        mayonnaise

Combine chicken, celery, red pepper, lemon juice, and salt. Add enough mayonnaise to hold mixture together.

Cover and chill for several hours.

Serves 4.

Cucumber Salad

If you like things spicy, add 1 teaspoon horseradish and 1 teaspoon lemon juice at the time you add the cucumber.

1	package (8 ounces) cream cheese, softened
1	package unflavored gelatin
2	cups diced cucumbers
1	cup mayonnaise
1/4	cup diced onion
1/4	cup fresh, chopped parsley
1/2	teaspoon salt
	lettuce

Combine cream cheese and mayonnaise. Mix well. Heat 1/4 cup of water to boiling. Remove from heat and add gelatin, stirring until dissolved. Add to cheese mixture. Add cucumbers, onion, parsley and salt. Pour into a 1-quart mold.

Chill for 3 hours or until set. Unmold onto lettuce.

Serves 6.

Grapefruit Salad

Goes well with chicken...

3	**envelopes unflavored gelatin**
1	**cup sugar**
3	**large grapefruits**
1	**cup blanched almonds**
1	**can (#2) crushed pineapple**
	fruit salad dressing or mayonnaise

Soften gelatin in 1 cup of cold water. Add to 1 cup of boiling water and stir until dissolved. Add sugar and stir until dissolved. Cut out sectioned grapefruit. Combine grapefruit sections, almonds, and pineapple (including juice) with gelatin mixture. Pour into a 1-quart mold and chill for 3 hours or until firm.

Serve with fruit salad dressing or mayonnaise.

Serves 6 to 8.

Greek Salad

This is really a meal by itself.

1	clove garlic, cut
6	cups romaine lettuce, washed and dried
2	medium tomatoes, cut into wedges
1	medium cucumber, peeled and sliced
1	green pepper, seeded and sliced
2	green onions, chopped
2	ounces feta cheese, cubed or crumbled
12	Greek olives
1	ounce flat anchovie fillets, drained

Dressing:

2	tablespoons olive oil
3	tablespoons lemon juice
1/4	teaspoon oregano
1/4	teaspoon mint
	freshly ground pepper to taste

Rub salad bowl with garlic clove. Combine romaine, tomatoes, cucumber, green pepper, onions, cheese, and olives in the bowl. Chill until ready to serve.

Prepare dressing by combining oil, lemon juice, oregano, mint, and pepper in a cruet. Shake well. Pour over salad and toss just before serving.

Serves 4.

Layered Salad

Prepare this the day before you want to use it!

3	cups shredded iceberg lettuce
1	cup sliced carrots
1	cup sliced cucumber
1	cup coarsely shredded red cabbage
4	cups cooked macaroni
3	hard cooked eggs, sliced
1	small purple onion, thinly sliced and separated into rings
1	cup julienne-sliced ham
1	package (10 ounces) frozen English peas, thawed and drained
1/2	cup shredded Cheddar cheese
1/2	cup shredded Monterey Jack cheese
2	tablespoons chopped fresh parsley

Dressing:

1	cup mayonnaise
1/2	cup sour cream
1/4	cup sliced green onions
2	teaspoons spicy prepared mustard
1	teaspoon sugar
1/4	teaspoon salt
1/4	teaspoon pepper

Layer lettuce, carrots, cucumber, cabbage, macaroni, eggs, onion, ham, peas, and cheeses in order listed above in a large salad bowl. To make the dressing, combine mayonnaise, sour cream, onions, mustard, sugar, salt and pepper, mixing well. Spread the dressing over the salad, sealing to the edge of the bowl.

Cover and chill for 8 hours. Sprinkle parsley over the top just before serving.

Serves 6.

Congealed Lobster Salad

You may want to substitute shrimp for the lobster or combine a little of both!

2	envelopes unflavored gelatin
1	cup tomato juice
1/2	cup tomato sauce
	juice from 1 large lemon
1	tablespoon Worchestershire sauce
1/4	cup white wine
2	tablespoons horseradish
1	large onion, minced
1/2	cup finely chopped celery
1/4	cup finely chopped green pepper
2	green onions, finely chopped
1	teaspoon chopped fresh parsley
2	cloves garlic, minced
	salt, pepper and red pepper to taste
1	pound lobster or 1 pound shrimp

Sauce:

3/4	cup mayonnaise
4	tablespoons horseradish sauce
1	tablespoon Worchestershire sauce
1/3	cup lemon juice
	salt and pepper to taste
1	teaspoon chopped fresh parsley

Soften gelatin in 1/2 cup cold water. Heat tomato juice to boiling. Remove from heat and add gelatin, stirring until dissolved. Add tomato sauce, lemon juice, Worchestershire sauce, wine, horseradish, onion, celery, green pepper, parsley, garlic, salt and pepper, stirring well. Break lobster into small pieces and add to mixture. Pour into a 1-quart oiled mold. Cover and chill until firm.

Prepare sauce by combining the mayonnaise, horseradish, Worchestershire sauce, lemon juice, salt, pepper and parsley. Unmold salad and serve with sauce.

Serves 8 to 10.

Mandarin Orange Salad

I like this with shrimp and crab dishes.

1	can (15 1/4 ounces) crushed pineapple
1	can (11 ounces) mandarine oranges
1	package (6 ounces) orange gelatin
1 1/2	cups hot tea
1	can (8 ounces) water chestnuts, drained and chopped
	lettuce
	fresh parsley

Dressing:

1/2	cup mayonnaise
1/4	cup whipping cream
1	tablespoon grated orange rind
1	teaspoon sugar
1/4	teaspoon ground mace

Drain pineapple and oranges and reserve juices. Add enough water to the juices to make 1 1/2 cups. Dissolve gelatin in the hot tea. Add reserved liquid and chill until partially set. Fold in pineapple, oranges, and water chestnuts. Spoon mixture into an oiled 6-cup mold. Cover and chill for 4 hours or until firm.

To make the dressing, combine mayonnaise, cream, orange rind, sugar and mace, stirring well. Unmold onto lettuce and fill center with a small amount of dressing. Garnish with parsley.

Serves 6 to 8.

German Potato Salad

This was Marnie Park's mother's recipe. Marnie is from Beaufort and Charlotte (NC).

1	**pound (3 medium) potatoes**
6	**slices bacon, diced**
2	**tablespoons diced onion**
1/2	**cup vinegar**
1/2	**cup stock or boullion**
1	**teaspoon salt**
1/4	**teaspoon pepper**
1	**teaspoon sugar**
1	**egg yolk, beaten**

Scrub potatoes. Boil in jackets and let cool. Peel and cut into 1/4 inch cubes. Cook bacon until crisp. Add onion and stir until transparent. Add vinegar, stock, salt, pepper, and sugar. Stir and let come to a boil. Stir in egg. Remove from heat and pour over potatoes.

Serve hot in a casserole.

Serves 2 to 4.

Red Potato Salad

My daughter, Jess McLamb of Raleigh (NC), is asked to make this at every family gathering.

2	pounds red new potatoes, scrubbed
1/2	cup diced onion
1	cup chopped celery
1	teaspoon celery seed
1 1/2	cups Italian dressing (prepared Good Seasons mix is best)
	salt, red pepper, and ground pepper to taste

Boil potatoes until tender. Drain. While still warm, cut into cubes (don't peel). Combine with onion, celery, celery seed, dressing, salt, red pepper, and ground pepper. Mix well.

This is best when served immediately while the potatoes are still warm. If not served immediately, you may need to add additional dressing.

Serves 6.

Raspberry Salad

This is a wonderfully tart salad.

1	**envelope unflavored gelatin**
1	**large package (6 ounces) raspberry gelatin**
1	**can (8 ounces) crushed pineapple**
1/2	**cup chopped pecans**
2	**packages (10 ounces each) frozen raspberries in syrup, thawed**
1	**container (8 ounces) sour cream**
	fresh parsley

Soften unflavored gelatin in 1/2 cup cold water. Bring 2 cups of water to boiling and add raspberry gelatin. Remove from heat and stir until dissolved. Combine with unflavored gelatin. Add pineapple, pecans, and raspberries, stirring well to break up fruit. Refrigerate until partially set. Spoon half of mixture into an 8-cup mold. Gently spread sour cream 1/2-inch thick over gelatin. Spoon remaining gelatin mixture over sour cream. Cover and refrigerate for 4 hours or until set.

Unmold onto a chilled platter and garnish with parsley.

Serves 10.

Romaine Salad with Pecans

This came from my daughter's sister-in-law, Mary Pritchard, of Winston-Salem (NC). It combines some unique flavors.

1	tablespoon butter or margarine
1	cup chopped pecans
3	heads romaine lettuce, cleaned and broken into pieces
1/2	cup thinly sliced red onion
2	cans (11 ounces) mandarin oranges, drained
1	cup croutons

Dressing:

1/4	cup lemon juice
1	teaspoon garlic salt
2	tablespoons grated Parmesan cheese
	salt and pepper to taste
3/4	cup light olive oil

Melt butter in a small skillet and add pecans. Saute for 3 to 4 minutes. Remove from skillet and drain on a paper towel. Place romaine, onions, and oranges in a large salad bowl. Cover and chill until ready to serve.

To make the dressing, combine lemon juice, garlic salt, cheese, salt, pepper and oil in a cruet. Shake well. Pour over salad just prior to serving. Toss well. Top with croutons.

Serves 10 to 12.

Romaine and Cheese Salad

I like this better than caesar salad

2	cloves garlic, cut into quarters
1/4	cup olive oil
2	small heads romaine lettuce (washed, dried and chilled)
1/2	cup Parmesan cheese
1/4	cup blue cheese
2	cups French bread cubes, toasted (4 slices bread)

Dressing:

6	tablespoons olive oil
3 1/2	tablespoons lemon juice
1/2	teaspoon salt
1/2	teaspoon pepper
1	egg
1	tablespoon Worchestershire sauce

Combine garlic and oil in a container and let stand for several hours at room temperature. Place the romaine in a large salad bowl. Sprinkle the cheeses over the romaine.

Prepare the dressing by combining the oil, lemon juice, salt, pepper, egg, and Worchestershire sauce in a jar. Cover and shake well. Pour over romaine and toss well. Remove garlic from the oil and pour the oil over the bread cubes. Add to salad and toss.

Serves 4 to 6.

Wilted Spinach Salad

A great summer lunch.

6	ounces fresh spinach, washed and dried
2	tablespoons bacon fat, slightly heated
2	tablespoons olive oil
4	teaspoons wine vinegar
1/2	teaspoon dry mustard
1	teaspoon soy sauce
1	tablespoon minced onion
1/4	teaspoon seasoned salt
8	slices crisp bacon, crumbled
1/4	cup garlic croutons

Remove stems from spinach leaves and break into bite-sized pieces. Set aside. Add bacon fat, olive oil, vinegar, mustard, soy sauce, onion, and salt to a large skillet. Heat through. Add bacon and half of the spinach. Toss well. Add remaining spinach and toss. Serve immediately.

Serves 4.

Tomato Soup Salad

Make this extra special by adding 1 pound of crabmeat or 1 pound of shrimp and leave out the nuts.

1	can (10 3/4 ounces) condensed tomato soup
1	package (8 ounces) cream cheese
2	packages unflavored gelatin
1	cup mayonnaise
2	tablespoons chopped green pepper
1/2	cup chopped pecans
1	cup finely chopped celery
1	teaspoon minced onions
	juice of 1/2 lemon

Heat tomato soup in a saucepan. Add cream cheese. Stir until cheese is melted. Dissolve gelatin in 1/2 cup cold water. Add to soup mixture. Remove from the heat and add mayonnaise, green pepper, pecans, celery, onions, and lemon juice. Mix well. Pour into an oiled 1-quart mold.

Cover and chill for 4 hours or until firm.

Serves 6.

Vegetable Molded Salad

This goes well with chicken or turkey.

1	large package (6 ounces) lemon gelatin
2	cups English peas
1	cup chopped carrots, cooked
1	cup chopped celery
1	teaspoon chopped green pepper
4	teaspoons vinegar
1	teaspoon sugar
1	teaspoon salt
1	teaspoon prepared mustard
1	tablespoon chopped onion
1	cup mayonnaise

Heat 1 1/2 cups water to boiling. Add gelatin and stir until dissolved. Cool. Add peas, carrots, celery, green pepper, vinegar, sugar, salt, mustard, onion and mayonnaise. Mix well. Pour into a 1-quart mold.

Cover and chill for 4 hours or until firm.

Serves 6.

Frozen Cranberry Salad

This goes well with your Thanksgiving or Christmas turkey.

1	**cup sour cream**
1	**package (3 ounces) cream cheese, softened**
1/2	**cup sugar**
2	**cans (16 ounces each) whole cranberry sauce**
1	**can (8 ounces) crushed pineapple, drained**
1	**cup chopped pecans**
1	**container (8 ounces) frozen whipped topping, thawed**
	fresh parsley

Combine sour cream, cream cheese, and sugar in a bowl and mix well with an electric mixer. Stir in cranberry sauce, pineapple, and pecans. Spoon mixture into an oiled 6-cup mold. Freeze at least overnight.

Just slightly thaw salad and garnish with parsley when serving.

Serves 6 to 8.

Frozen Fruit Salad

Keep in your freezer for "drop in" guests. It goes well with whatever you are serving.

1	can (16 ounces) apricot halves, drained
1	can (16 ounces) pineapple chunks, drained
1	can (16 ounces) sliced peaches, drained
1	can (16 ounces) pear halves, drained and sliced
1	can (16 ounces) fruit cocktail, drained
1	cup chopped pecans
1	package (10 1/2 ounces) miniature marshmallows
1	pint whipping cream, whipped
1/2	cup plus 4 teaspoons mayonnaise
1	small jar (6 ounces) marachino cherries, drained

Combine apricots, pineapple, peaches, pears, fruit cocktail, pecans, marshmallows, whipped cream, and 1/2 cup mayonnaise. Mix thoroughly. Spoon into individual molds and place a cherry on top of each mold. Cover tightly with saran wrap, then aluminum foil and freeze for at least 6 hours before serving.

Serve frozen with a dollop of mayonnaise.

Serves 10 to 12.

Fruits and
Vegetables

Asparagus Casserole

This recipe is a favorite of my mother, Mrs. Helen Jones, and our entire family!

3	tablespoons butter or margarine
4	tablespoons all-purpose flour
2	cups milk
3/4	cup grated sharp Cheddar cheese
1/2	teaspoon salt
	paprika
2	hard boiled eggs, sliced
2	cans green asparagus, drained
1	cup buttered bread crumbs (enough to cover top of baking dish)

Preheat oven to 350 degrees.

Melt butter in saucepan. Stir in flour until smooth. Gradually add milk, stirring constantly until thickened. Remove from heat and season with salt and paprika.

Lightly oil a 2-quart baking dish. Layer sauce, asparagus and sliced eggs in the dish. Pour sauce over the layers. Cover with bread crumbs.

Cover and bake for 1 hour.

Serves 6.

Artichoke and Asparagus Strata

Wendy Park, co-owner of the Beaufort Grocery Co. (a popular eatery in Beaufort, NC), shared this.

2	cups diced stale white bread
2	cups shredded provolone or Swiss cheese
2	tablespoons butter or margarine
1	leek, sliced thin
1 1/2	cups sliced fresh mushrooms
1	cup artichoke hearts, drained and chopped
1	cup chopped asparagus
6	eggs, beaten in a large bowl
1/4	cup white wine
1 1/2	cups milk
	salt and pepper to taste
1	tablespoon mixed fresh herbs (use a combination of dill, parsley, basil, etc. - whatever you have on hand)

Preheat oven to 350 degrees.

Butter a 9" x 13" pan. Put bread in the bottom and sprinkle half of the cheese on the bread. Saute leeks in butter until soft, then add mushrooms, artichoke hearts, and asparagus. Saute until warm. Spread vegetable mixture over the bread and cheese. Sprinkle the remaining cheese on top.

In a large bowl, mix together the eggs, wine, milk, salt and pepper, and herbs. Pour over the cheese and shake the pan to make sure that the liquid soaks to the bottom. Bake for 1 hour. Cut into squares and serve hot.

Serves 4 to 6.

Baked Beans

These go great with hamburgers and hot dogs.

1	pound Great Northern dried beans
1/4	pound salt pork, diced, plus 1/4 pound, sliced
1	large onion, chopped
3/4	cup light brown sugar
1/2	cup catsup
1	teaspoon dry mustard
2	teaspoons salt
1	tablespoon Worchestershire sauce

Place beans in a large bowl and cover with cold water. Cover dish and place in the refrigerator overnight.

Next day: Drain beans. Place beans in a large saucepan and cover with cold water. Bring to a boil, then reduce heat and simmer about 1 hour or until the skins of the beans start to burst. Drain.

Preheat oven to 275 degrees.

Lightly oil a 3-quart casserole dish. Pour beans into the dish. Add diced pork, onion, sugar, catsup, mustard, salt, Worchestershire sauce and 1 cup boiling water. Mix well. Arrange strips of pork on top. Cover and bake for 5 hours. Uncover and bake for 1 more hour.

Note: Add more water if beans become too dry.

Serves 8.

Green Bean Casserole I

This is the traditional version of this "old standby" and versatile side dish.

2	cans (16 ounces each) French style green beans, drained
1	can (6 ounces) French fried onions
1	can (8 ounces) sliced water chestnuts, drained
1	can (10 3/4 ounces) cream of mushroom soup

Preheat oven to 350 degrees.

Combine beans, 3/4 of the onions, and water chestnuts in a greased 1-quart casserole. Stir in mushroom soup. Sprinkle with remaining onions. Bake about 20 minutes or until brown and bubbly.

Serves 6.

Green Bean Casserole II

If you like cheese, this is a slight variation from the traditional version.

2	cans (16 ounces each) French style green beans
1/4	cup butter or margarine
1	cup grated sharp Cheddar cheese
1	pint sour cream
1	cup toasted bread crumbs

Preheat oven to 400 degrees.

Pour beans into a saucepan and cook for 15 minutes. Drain. Add butter, cheese, sour cream, and half of the bread crumbs. Pour into a greased 1 /12-quart casserole dish. Place the remaining bread crumbs on top. Bake until brown and bubbly.

Serves 4.

Brocolli Casserole

This recipe was a favorite of my chef, Cora Davis, at the Kinston Country Club.

2	large onions, chopped
10	large fresh mushrooms
1/4	cup butter or margarine
6	packages (10 ounces each) frozen chopped brocolli
4	cups (2 cans - 10 3/4 ounces each) cream of mushroom soup
3	packages (6 ounces each) garlic cheese
2	teaspoons MSG (optional)
1	cup chopped blanched almonds
1	cup bread crumbs

Saute onions and mushrooms in butter. Add brocolli and cook until tender. Add mushroom soup, cheese, MSG, and 3/4 cup almonds. Pour into 2 2-quart greased casserole dishes. Sprinkle remaining almonds and bread crumbs on top. Bake until brown and bubbly.

Serves 18.

Brocolli with Fresh Orange Sauce

Sometimes, it's fun to get "fancy" with the brocolli.

1	**bunch fresh brocolli**
2	**tablespoons butter or margarine**
2	**tablespoons all-purpose flour**
1/2	**teaspoon grated fresh orange peel**
1/2	**cup fresh orange juice (from 2 medium oranges)**
1/2	**cup sour cream**
1/4	**teaspoon thyme**
1/2	**teaspoon salt**
1/8	**teaspoon pepper**

Wash brocolli and remove large leaves and tough parts of stalks. Separate into individual spears. Place in a large saucepan with 1/2 inch boiling water. Cover pan and simmer 10 to 12 minutes.

Melt butter in small saucepan. Blend in flour. Stir in orange peel, orange juice, sour cream, thyme, salt and pepper. Stir over low heat until mixture thickens and comes to a boil.

Drain cooked brocolli and serve with sauce.

Serves 4.

Cabbage Casserole

Mary Louise Wooten from Kinston (NC) gave this one to me.

1	medium head cabbage, diced
1	tablespoon bacon grease
	salt to taste
1	teaspoon baking powder
1	egg, beaten
1	cup bread crumbs

Preheat oven to 350 degrees.

Place cabbage in a large saucepan. Cover with water and add bacon grease and salt. Let water come to a boil, then simmer until tender. Drain cabbage. Add baking powder, egg, and bread crumbs. Place mixture in a 1 1/2-quart greased baking dish and bake for 15 or 20 minutes.

Serves 6.

German Red Cabbage

This is great with pork chops or corned beef.

2/3	cup red wine vinegar
2	tablespoons sugar
2	teaspoons salt
3	pounds red cabbage, shredded
2	slices of bacon
2	tablespoons bacon drippings
3	medium Granny Smith apples, cut into 1/8 inch wedges
1/2	cup finely chopped onions
1	whole onion, peeled and pierced with 2 whole cloves
4	tablespoons dry red wine
4	tablespoons red currant jelly

Combine sugars, salt and vinegar, stirring until sugar and salt dissolves. Pour over cabbage and toss to coat. Let stand 5 to 10 minutes.

Cook bacon until crisp. Remove bacon, reserving drippings. Crumble bacon and set aside.

In a Dutch oven, add bacon drippings, apples and chopped onion. Saute until lightly browned, approximately 5 minutes. Add cabbage, whole onion, and bay leaf. Stir thoroughly.

Pour in 2 cups of boiling water. Return to boil, reduce heat, cover and simmer for 45 minutes to 1 hour, stirring occasionally. Keep moist while simmering, but there should be almost no water left in the pan when done.

Remove onion and bay leaf. Stir in wine and currant jelly. Spoon into a serving dish and sprinkle bacon on top.

Serves 6 to 8.

Scalloped Cabbage

Try something a little different with cabbage ...

1	medium cabbage, cored and chopped
4	tablespoon butter or margarine
1/4	cup chopped onion
1/4	cup chopped green pepper
1	cup shredded sharp Cheddar cheese, divided
3	tablespoons all-purpose flour
1 1/2	cups milk
3/4	teaspoons salt
	dash of pepper
1/2	cup bread crumbs

Preheat oven to 350 degrees.

Cook cabbage for 10 minutes in about 1 cup boiling, salted water. Drain.

Saute onion and pepper in 1 tablespoon of butter until tender. Place half of the cabbage in a 2 1/2-quart casserole, top with onions, pepper and half the cheese. Top with remaining cabbage and cheese.

Make a white sauce by melting 3 tablespoons of butter in a small pan and stirring in the flour. When well mixed, add milk gradually. Cook, stirring constantly, until thick. Add salt and pepper and pour over the casserole. Sprinkle with bread crumbs. Bake for 25 minutes.

Serves 8.

Carrots Amandine

Sometimes you have to dress it up to entice people to eat it!

1	**pound carrots, peeled and thinly sliced**
1/4	**cup golden raisins**
1/4	**cup butter or margarine**
3	**tablespoon honey**
1	**tablespoon lemon juice**
1/4	**teaspoon ground ginger**
1/4	**cup sliced almonds**

Preheat oven to 375 degrees.

Cook carrots, covered in 1/2 inch boiling water for 8 minutes. Drain. Turn carrots into a 1-quart baking dish. Stir in raisins, butter, honey, lemon juice, and ginger. Bake, uncovered, for 35 minutes. Spoon into a serving bowl and sprinkle with almonds.

Serves 4.

Carrot Souffle

This really makes the carrot special.

2	cups cooked, pureed carrots (puree, then measure)
2	teaspoons fresh lemon juice
2	tablespoons minced onions
1/2	cup butter or margarine, softened
1/4	cup sugar
1	tablespoon self-rising flour
1	teaspoon salt
1/4	teaspoon cinnamon
1	cup milk
3	eggs

Preheat oven to 350 degrees.

Combine carrot puree and lemon juice in a large mixing bowl. Beat in onion, butter, sugar, flour, salt, and cinnamon. Add milk. Mix well. Add eggs, one at a time, and mix thoroughly. Pour into a greased 2-quart casserole and bake for 1 1/2 hours.

Serves 4 to 5.

Marinated Carrots

These are good for "nibbling" and they will keep in the refrigerator for at least a week.

2	pounds medium carrots, sliced
1	small green pepper, chopped
1	medium onion, thinly sliced
1/4	cup lemon juice
1	teaspoon salt
1	cup sugar
1/2	cup vinegar
1/2	cup salad oil
1	can (10 3/4 ounces) condensed tomato soup
1	teaspoon dry mustard
1	teaspoon Worchestershire sauce
3/4	teaspoon pepper

Peel and slice carrots. Cook until just tender. Cool in cold water. Drain. Arrange in a glass container with a lid.

Combine onion, lemon juice, salt, sugar, vinegar, salad oil, tomato soup, mustard, Worchestershire sauce, and pepper. Mix well. Pour over carrots.

Place container in the refrigerator over night.

Serves 4 to 6.

Cauliflower with Cheese Sauce

This is good with any dinner menu.

1	head cauliflower
3	tablespoons butter or margarine
3	tablespoons all-purpose flour
1	cup milk
1/2	teaspoon salt
	dash of pepper
1 1/2	cups grated sharp Cheddar cheese

Preheat oven to 350 degrees.

Wash cauliflower and break into flowerettes. Boil cauliflower until almost done (still crispy). Melt butter in a small saucepan. Stir in flour. Add milk gradually. Stir in salt and pepper. Cook over low heat until thickened. Blend in cheese. Simmer until cheese is melted, stirring constantly.

Place cauliflower in a greased 1 1/2-quart baking dish. Pour cheese mixture over cauliflower. Bake about 15 minutes.

Serves 4.

Creole Celery

This is especially good with seafood.

1	**tablespoon butter or margarine**
2	**cups sliced celery**
1/4	**cup chopped onion**
3/4	**teaspoon salt**
1/8	**teaspoon pepper**
1 1/2	**cups canned tomatoes, drained**
2	**tablespoons chopped fresh parsley**

Melt butter in saucepan. Add celery, onion, salt and pepper. Cover and simmer for 10 minutes. Add tomatoes. Continue to cook for 5 minutes or until celery is done and tomatoes are hot. Add parsley and serve.

Serves 4.

fresh Corn Pudding

Erwin Parrott from Kinston (NC) contributed this easy-to-fix corn dish that was her mother's favorite.

4	eggs
1	can (16 ounces) cream-style corn
1	cup milk
1	tablespoon butter or margarine, melted
1	tablespoon all-purpose flour
	salt and pepper to taste
1	teaspoon sugar

Preheat oven to 350 degrees.

Beat eggs in a medium mixing bowl. Add corn, milk, butter, and flour, stirring well. Season with salt, pepper and sugar. Pour mixture into a greased 1-quart casserole dish and bake for 30 minutes or until mixture is set.

Serves 4 to 6.

Corn Souffle

Another treat from my mother's kitchen... a year-round favorite of corn lovers.

1/2	cup (2 sticks) butter or margarine
1/4	cup sugar
1	tablespoon all-purpose flour
1/2	cup light cream or evaporated milk
2	eggs, well beaten
1 1/2	teaspoons baking powder
	salt to taste
4	cups frozen uncooked corn, thawed or fresh corn
	cinnamon to taste

Preheat oven to 350 degrees.

Heat butter in a medium saucepan until melted. Stir in sugar and flour. Remove from heat. Gradually stir in cream. Add eggs, baking powder and salt. Mix well. Fold in corn. Pour mixture into a 2-quart greased casserole dish. Bake for 45 minutes.

Sprinkle with cinnamon before serving.

Serves 6.

Cranberry-Apple Casserole

This is a great side dish with turkey or pork. You can prepare it early and bake it just before serving.

4	cups apples, sliced
2	cups fresh cranberries
1	cup sugar
1/2	cup brown sugar
1	cup oatmeal, uncooked (regular or instant is OK)
1	stick butter or margarine, melted

Preheat oven to 350 degrees.

Grease a 1-quart baking dish. Arrange apples and cranberries in dish. Sprinkle sugar over the fruit, then cover with oatmeal. Drizzle butter over the oatmeal. Bake for 45 minutes.

Serves 4 to 6.

Eggplant Casserole

I got this variation of the traditional eggplant casserole from Aunt Jess Heller from New Milford (CT).

1	medium eggplant, peeled and cubed
2	medium onions, finely chopped
2	stalks celery, finely chopped
1/4	cup finely chopped green pepper
	salt to taste
1	cup tomato sauce
2	cups shredded sharp Cheddar cheese
3/4	cup corn chips

Preheat oven to 350 degrees.

Combine eggplant, onion, celery, and green pepper in large frying pan. Just barely cover with water and add salt to taste. Cook mixture until tender. Drain. Add tomato sauce. Combine cheese and corn chips in a bowl, tossing well.

Spoon eggplant mixture into a greased 1 1/2-quart casserole dish. Stir in half of the cheese mixture. Top with remaining cheese mixture. Bake for 30 minutes.

Serves 8.

Eggplant Lasagna Casserole

If you want to cut down on red meat, try this version of the traditional lasagna.

2	medium-sized eggplants (about 1 1/2 pounds each)
6	tablespoons olive or salad oil
1	small onion, chopped
2	teaspoons sugar
1 1/2	teaspoons salt
1	teaspoon dried basil leaves
2	cans (28 ounces) tomatoes and liquid
2/3	package (16 ounces) lasagna noodles (about 12 noodles)
1/4	cup grated Parmesan cheese
1	package (8 ounces) shredded mozzarella cheese (2 cups)

Preheat oven to broil.

About 1 1/2 hours before serving, preheat broiler. Peel and slice eggplants crosswise into 1/4 inch thick slices. Place half of slices on rack in broiling pan. Brush both sides of slices with 2 tablespoons oil. Broil slices 10 minutes or until browned, turning eggplant once halfway through cooking time. Repeat with remaining eggplant slices and 2 tablespoons oil. Change oven setting to 375 degrees.

While eggplants are broiling, prepare tomato sauce. In a 4-quart saucepan, add 2 tablespoons oil and onions. Saute until tender. Stir in sugar, salt, basil, and tomatoes (and their liquid). Heat to boiling, stirring to break up the tomatoes. Reduce heat to low. Simmer, uncovered, for 15 minutes. Stir occasionally.

Prepare lasagna noodles following directions on the package. Drain. In a 13" x 9" baking dish, evenly spoon 1 cup tomato sauce. Arrange half of the noodles over the sauce, overlapping to fit. Arrange half of the eggplant slices over the noodles. Top with half of the Parmesan and mozzarella cheese. Repeat the layers. Bake the lasagna 40 minutes or until heated through and noodles are tender. Remove from oven and let stand for 10 minutes for easier serving.

Serves 10.

Onion Pie

Can you imagine an onion pie? It's really good. Try it as a "first course."

1	stick butter or margarine
5	medium sweet onions (Vadalia or Walla Walla, if available), sliced
1/4	teaspoon salt
1/4	teaspoon pepper
2	dashes Tabasco sauce
1/4	teaspoon dry mustard
3	eggs, well beaten
1	cup sour cream
1	9-inch deep-dish pastry shell, unbaked
1/2	cup grated sharp Cheddar cheese

Preheat oven to 450 degrees.

Heat butter in a frying pan. Add onions and saute until the onions are clear, but not brown. Combine salt, pepper, Tabasco sauce, mustard, eggs, and sour cream in a medium size bowl and mix well. Stir in the onions. Pour the mixture into the pastry shell and top with cheese. Bake for 20 minutes, then reduce the oven temperature to 325 degrees. Continue baking until the filling is set and the top is golden brown, approximately 20 more minutes.

Let cool for at least 10 minutes before cutting into serving pieces.

Makes 12 servings.

Onion Rings

My son-in-law, Gene McLamb of Raleigh, loves these. They're great with steak or just indulging.

3	large Bermuda onions (about 3 pounds)
2	eggs, lightly beaten
2	cups buttermilk
2	cups all-purpose flour
1	teaspoon baking soda
2	teaspoons salt
	fat for deep frying
	salt to taste

Peel, then slice onions into 1/4 inch slices and break into individual rings. Soak in large bowl(s) filled with ice-cold water at least 1 hour, until fully chilled (this makes the rings crispy).

Beat eggs with buttermilk, then stir in flour, baking soda, and salt. Heat fat in a large skillet or deep fat fryer to 350 degrees.

Remove a few onion rings from ice water and thoroughly pat dry. Dip in buttermilk batter, let excess drip off. Fry in fat, turning once, until golden brown. Do not crowd in deep fryer. Drain rings on paper towels and keep warm in 200-degree oven. Continue frying onion rings, a few at a time. Serve as soon as possible.

Salt to taste and serve immediately.

Serves 4 to 6.

Baked Onions

This is another of Alice Wheatly's goodies. She keeps us well fed in Beaufort (NC).

Onions:
8   medium (3 pounds) yellow onions
4   chicken bouillon cubes
3   tablespoons butter or margarine, melted
1/2   teaspoon paprika
         dash of pepper

Crumb topping:
1/3   cup packaged dry bread crumbs
2   tablespoons butter or margarine, melted
1/2   teaspoon salt
1/8   teaspoon thyme

Peel onions. Place in a large saucepan, along with bouillon cubes and 2 quarts of water. Bring to a boil. Reduce heat and simmer, covered, for 30 minutes or until onions are tender. Drain.

Preheat oven to 400 degrees.

Line a shallow baking pan with foil. Place butter, paprika, and pepper in foil-lined pan. Add onions and toss to coat well with butter. Bake 10 minutes.

While onions are cooking, make the crumb topping. In a small bowl, combine crumbs, butter, salt, and thyme. Sprinkle over top of onions. Bake onion mixture with topping for an additional 10 minutes.

Serves 8.

Noodles Amandine

This is especially great with any veal dish.

1/2	**cup slivered almonds**
1/2	**pound fresh mushrooms**
9	**tablespoons butter or margarine**
2	**tablespoons grated onion**
6	**tablespoons all-purpose flour**
2	**cups milk**
1/2	**teaspoon salt**
	dash of pepper
1	**package (12 ounces) egg noodles**
3/4	**cup grated Swiss cheese or sharp Cheddar cheese**

Saute almonds in 1 tablespoon of butter until crisp and brown. Slice mushrooms thin and saute in 2 tablespoons of butter for 3 minutes, stirring frequently. Add onions.

Prepare cream sauce: Melt 6 tablespoons of butter in a small saucepan, stir in flour, then add milk gradually. Stir in salt and pepper. Cook over low heat until thickened.

Combine almonds and mushroom mixture. Gradually stir in cream sauce.

Cook noodles as directed on package. Drain. Toss noodles with sauce. Serve on heated platter and sprinkle with cheese.

Serves 6

Green Pea Casserole

The stuffing mix makes the difference in this one.

1	package frozen peas
1	stick butter or margarine
2	medium onions, chopped
4	ounces (8 medium size) fresh mushrooms
1	stalk celery, chopped
1/2	tablespoon all-purpose flour
1	can sliced water chestnuts
	salt and pepper to taste
1	(8 ounces) Pepperidge Farm Stuffing mix
1	teaspoon soy sauce

Preheat oven to 350 degrees.

Cook peas following directions on package and drain. Saute onions, mushrooms, and celery in 3/4 stick butter. Add flour. Remove from heat and add peas, water chestnuts, salt and pepper. Place in greased 1-quart baking dish. Cover with stuffing mix. Dot with remaining butter. Bake for 25 minutes or until bubbly.

Serves 4.

Pepper Souffle

Yvonne Brakebill, from Raleigh (NC), shared this versatile recipe that can be used as a side dish or as an hors d'oeurve.

2	cans (4 ounces) chopped green chili peppers
1	pound sharp Cheddar cheese, grated
3	cups milk
1	cup Bisquick mix
3	eggs, beaten

Preheat oven to 350 degrees.

Place peppers in greased 9" x 9" baking dish and top with cheese. Blend milk and Bisquick. Add eggs and blend well. Pour batter over peppers and cheese mixture. Bake for 1 hour.

Serves 4 to 6.

Cheddar Baked Potato Slices

Cheese and potatoes make a great duo.

1	can (10 3/4 ounce) cream of mushroom soup
1/2	teaspoon paprika
1/2	teaspoon pepper
4	medium baking potatoes, cut into 1/4" slices (about 4 cups)
1	cup shredded sharp Cheddar cheese

Preheat oven to 400 degrees.

Combine soup, paprika, and pepper in a small bowl. Set aside. Arrange potatoes (in overlapping rows) in a greased 2-quart oblong baking dish. Sprinkle with cheese. Spoon soup mixture over potatoes. Cover with foil and bake for 45 minutes. Uncover and bake for 10 more minutes or until potatoes are tender.

Makes 6 servings.

Potato-Cabbage Dish

This is a unique combination and really good.

1 1/2	pounds potatoes, peeled and cubed
2	cups cabbage, finely chopped
1/4	cup chopped green onions
3	tablespoons butter or margarine
2	tablespoons fresh lime juice
1/8	teaspoon pepper
2	tablespoons chopped fresh parsley
1/4	teaspoon salt

Cook potatoes in 1 inch of boiling water for 10 to 15 minutes. Drain thoroughly. While potatoes are cooking, saute cabbage and onions in butter for 7 to 8 minutes or until tender, but not brown. Add potatoes, lime juice, pepper, parsley, and salt. Toss well.

Serve very hot.

Serves 6 to 8.

Potato Casserole

This can be made ahead and frozen.

5	pounds medium baking potatoes, peeled and cut into quarters
	salt to taste
1	container (8 ounces) whipped cream cheese with chives
1	teaspoon garlic salt
1/4	teaspoon pepper
6	tablespoons butter or margarine
2	cups heavy cream or whipping cream
1/4	cup sliced almonds
	paprika

About 1 1/2 hours before serving, place potatoes in a large saucepan with enough water to cover the potatoes. Add 1 teaspoon of salt. Cover and bring to a boil. Reduce to low heat. Simmer for 20 more minutes or until potatoes are tender. Drain well.

Preheat oven to 375 degrees.

Combine potatoes, cream cheese, garlic salt, pepper, 4 tablespoons of butter, and 1 teaspoon salt in a large bowl. Mash until smooth. Gradually add heavy cream, mixing well. Spoon potatoes into a greased 13" x 9" glass baking dish or shallow 3-quart casserole dish. Dot potatoes with 2 tablespoons butter. Sprinkle with almonds and paprika. Freeze at this point, if desired. Bake 30 minutes or until top is golden.

Makes 12 servings.

Duchesse Potatoes

An easy way to make potatoes look fancy.

---

6   medium baking potatoes
3   egg yolks
1   cup milk
       salt and pepper to taste

Preheat oven to 400 degrees.

Boil potatoes in enough water to cover, until tender. Peel potatoes and mash. Add egg yolks, one at a time, to hot potatoes. Beat well after adding each egg. Add enough milk to make potato mixture smooth (like mashed potatoes). Add salt and pepper. Place small mounds of potatoes (1 large serving spoon full) on a lightly greased baking sheet. Bake until brown.

Serve immediately.

Serves 6.

Escalloped Potatoes

Great with meatloaf or any beef and so easy to prepare!

6	large baking potatoes, peeled and sliced thinly
	salt and pepper to taste
	self-rising flour
2	large onions, peeled and thinly sliced
	butter or margarine
	milk

Preheat oven to 350 degrees.

In a 2-quart greased casserole dish, place a layer of potato slices. Sprinkle salt and pepper and a dusting of flour over the potatoes. Cover potatoes with a thin layer of onions. Dot with butter. Repeat layers of potatoes, salt, pepper, flour, onions and butter until the casserole dish is almost full. Pour enough milk into casserole to almost cover the mixture. Bake for 45 minutes or until potatoes are tender.

Serves 4 to 6.

Herb Stuffed Potatoes

These can be fixed ahead and heated just before serving.

6	**medium baking potatoes**
	vegetable oil
1/2	**cup butter or margarine**
1	**tablespoon finely chopped onion**
1	**tablespoon chopped fresh parsley**
1/2	**cup evaporated milk**
1/4	**teaspoon crushed basil leaves**
1/4	**teaspoon crushed tarragon leaves**
1	**teaspoon salt**
1/4	**teaspoon pepper**
	butter or margarine or grated sharp Cheddar cheese

Preheat oven to 400 degrees.

Scrub potatoes thoroughly and rub with oil. Bake potatoes for 1 hour or until done. Allow potatoes to cool to the touch.

Preheat oven to 350 degrees.

Slice skin away from the top of each potato. Carefully scoop out pulp, leaving shells intact. Mash pulp. Add 1/2 cup butter, onion, parsley, milk, and seasonings to potato pulp. Mix well. Stuff shells with potato mixture and dot the tops with butter or sprinkle with cheese. You can wrap well and freeze at this point, if desired. Bake for about 30 minutes.

Serves 6.

Potato Crunch

This is good with any meat dish.

1	**stick butter or margarine, melted**
4	**large russet potatoes**
1	**cup crushed cornflakes**
1	**cup grated sharp Cheddar cheese**
1 1/2	**teaspoons salt**
	paprika and pepper, if desired

Preheat oven to 375 degrees.

Pour butter in a large baking pan to cover the bottom. Slice potatoes 1/2 inch thick (peel, if desired). Place in a single layer in butter and turn once to coat.

Mix cornflake crumbs, cheese and salt and sprinkle on potatoes. Sprinkle paprika and pepper. Bake for 30 minutes or until potatoes are tender and topping is crisp.

Serves 3 to 4.

Sherried Sweet Potatoes

This is a Thanksgiving special.

1	can (28 ounces) sweet potatoes, drained
1/2	cup brown sugar
1/2	teaspoon cinnamon
1	stick butter or margarine
1/3	cup sherry
1/4	cup chopped pecans

Preheat oven to 350 degrees.

Pour potatoes into a greased 1-quart casserole dish. Sprinkle sugar and cinnamon over potatoes. Dot with butter and pour sherry over mixture. Sprinkle pecans on top. Bake for 45 minutes.

Serves 4.

Sweet Potato Pudding

My daughter, Jess McLamb, from Raleigh (NC) makes this every Thanksgiving. The topping makes the difference.

1/8	teaspoon nutmeg
1/8	teaspoon allspice
1/8	teaspoon ground cloves
1/8	teaspoon ground ginger
1/4	teaspoon cinnamon
	pinch of salt
1/2	cup sugar
1/2	teaspoon vanilla
1/2	stick butter or margarine, melted
3/4	cup milk
4	cups cooked, mashed sweet potatoes (about 7 medium potatoes)

Topping:
1	stick butter or margarine, melted
2 1/2	cups brown sugar
1	cup chopped pecans

Preheat oven to 350 degrees.

Combine nutmeg, allspice, cloves, ginger, cinnamon, salt, sugar, vanilla, and butter in a large mixing bowl. Beat well with a spoon. Add milk. Stir in potatoes. Mix well and pour into a greased 9" x 13" baking dish.

Combine butter, brown sugar and pecans to make the topping. Mixture should be crumbly. Sprinkle over top of casserole. Bake for 30 minutes or until bubbling.

Serves 12.

Rice Pilaf

Onions and mushrooms make everything taste a little better. This dish is no exception. This came from daughter, Jess McLamb.

1	**stick butter or margarine**
1	**medium onion, diced**
1	**can beef broth**
1	**cup uncooked rice**
1	**package (8 ounces) fresh mushrooms, cleaned and sliced**

Melt butter in medium size saucepan. Add onions, broth, rice, and mushrooms. Cover and cook at low to medium heat for 30 minutes or until rice is done.

Serves 6.

Chinese Fried Rice

Try with Chinese chicken stir fry - it's a winner.

1	**tablespoon oil**
2	**cups coarsely chopped onion**
1	**green pepper, chopped fine**
2	**celery stalks, chopped fine**
1	**cup shrimp, cooked and chopped**
3	**eggs, slightly beaten**
1	**tablespoon soy sauce**
1/2	**teaspoon salt**
1	**can sliced water chestnuts, drained**
1	**small can bamboo shoots, drained**
2	**cups cooked rice, cold**

Heat pan or wok. Add oil. Fry onions, peppers, and celery for 2 minutes. Add shrimp. Add eggs. Season with soy sauce and salt. Toss until eggs are cooked. Add water chestnuts, bamboo shoots, and rice. Saute until done.

Serves 6.

Subgum Fried Rice

This is a meal by itself.

4	**cups cold cooked rice**
3	**eggs, beaten**
1 1/2	**teaspoons salt**
3	**tablespoons oil**
3	**green onions**
1	**cup diced cooked chicken**
1	**cup diced cooked ham**
1/2	**cup frozen peas, thawed but not cooked**
1/4	**teaspoon pepper**
2	**tablespoons soy sauce**

Separate grains of rice as best you can. Beat eggs slightly and season with 1/2 teaspoon salt. Pour into 1 tablespoon of oil and scramble as you would breakfast eggs. Set aside to use later. Finely chop onions, using some of the green tops. Heat remaining 2 tablespoons of oil. Add onions and fry for a few seconds. Add rice and stir until heated through. Mix in chicken, ham, peas, 1 teaspoon salt, and pepper. Be sure mixture is heated through. Lightly toss in scrambled eggs and sprinkle with soy sauce.

Serves 4.

Squash Casserole

Squash is good year round.

2 to 3	pounds yellow squash, sliced
	salt and pepper to taste
1/2	cup butter or margarine, melted
1	cup sour cream
1	can (10 3/4 ounces) cream of chicken soup, undiluted
2	onions, finely chopped
1	can (5 ounces) sliced water chestnuts, drained
1	jar (2 ounces) pimentos, drained
1	package (8 ounces) herb-seasoned stuffing mix, divided

Preheat oven to 350 degrees.

Cook squash in boiling water until tender. Drain, reserving 1 1/2 cups liquid. Add salt and pepper. Mash. Combine reserved liquid and butter, sour cream, soup, onions, water chestnuts, pimentos, and all but 1/2 cup of the stuffing mix. Stir in squash.

Pour mixture into greased 2 1/2-quart casserole. Top with reserved stuffing mix. Bake for 30 minutes.

Serves 8.

Yellow Squash Souffle

Try this with pork.

1/4	cup butter or margarine
1/4	cup all-purpose flour
1 1/3	cups milk
1/2	teaspoon salt
	dash of red pepper
1	tablespoon minced onion
1 1/4	cups grated yellow squash (about 1 pound)
5	eggs, separated
1	teaspoon cream of tartar
1/2	cup (2 ounces) shredded sharp Cheddar cheese

Preheat oven to 350 degrees.

Melt butter in a heavy saucepan over low heat. Add flour, stirring until smooth. Cook 1 minute, stirring constantly. Gradually add milk. Cook over medium heat, stirring constantly, until thickened and bubbly. Stir in salt, pepper, and onion. Remove from heat and let cool.

Squeeze grated squash in paper towels to remove as much liquid as possible. Stir squash into sauce.

Beat egg yolks until thick and lemon colored. Add to squash mixture and stir well.

Beat egg whites (at room temperature) and cream of tartar until stiff but not dry. Fold into squash mixture. Pour into a greased 2-quart souffle dish. Bake for 1 hour. Sprinkle cheese on top and bake an additional 5 minutes or until a knife inserted in center comes out clean. Serve immediately.

Serves 6 to 8.

Spinach Rockefeller

A fancy presentation for spinach.

2	large packages (10 ounces each) chopped spinach, cooked and drained
2	cups bread crumbs
1	medium onion, diced and sauteed
6	eggs, beaten
3/4	cups butter or margarine, melted
1/2	cup grated Parmesan cheese
1	tablespoon Accent (optional)
1/2	tablespoon thyme
1	teaspoon pepper
1/2	teaspoon cayenne pepper
	salt to taste
12	medium size tomatoes
	garlic salt to taste

Preheat oven to 325 degrees.

Mix spinach, bread crumbs, onion, eggs, butter, cheese, and seasonings. Scoop out pulp from tomatoes. Sprinkle garlic salt inside each tomato. Fill each tomato with spinach mixture. Bake on buttered cookie sheet for 15 minutes.

Serves 12.

Cheesy Spinach Casserole

You won't even know you're eating something good for you.

2	packages (10 ounce) frozen chopped spinach
1	container (8 ounce) sour cream
2	tablespoons dry onion soup mix
1	cup (4 ounces) shredded medium Cheddar cheese

Cook spinach according to package directions, omitting salt. Drain well. Combine spinach, sour cream, and soup mix. Mix well. Spoon into a lightly greased 1-quart casserole. Sprinkle cheese over spinach mixture. Cover and chill overnight.

Remove casserole from the refrigerator 30 minutes before baking.

Preheat oven to 350 degrees.

Bake for 30 minutes.

Serves 6.

Scalloped Tomatoes

This dish is good with any fish or meat.

2	cups thinly sliced onions
5	tablespoons butter or margarine
1	tablespoon sugar
1	teaspoon salt
2 1/2	cups canned tomatoes
1/2	cup soft bread cubes
1/2	cup bread crumbs
1/4	cup grated sharp Cheddar cheese

Preheat oven to 350 degrees.

Melt 4 tablespoons butter in saucepan. Stir in onions. Add sugar and salt. Cook over low heat for 15 minutes. Do not brown. Arrange onions in a greased 1 1/2-quart baking dish. Mix tomatoes and soft bread cubes together gently and add to baking dish. Melt additional butter and add bread crumbs. Stir well to coat. Sprinkle bread crumbs and cheese over tomato mixture. Bake for 20 minutes or until brown.

Serves 6.

Fried Tomatoes

Cousin Hazel White from Norfolk (VA) rarely cooked (she lived with her mother) but she loved to cook these tomatoes!

	salt and pepper to taste
1	**cup corn meal**
	bacon grease
3	**green or firm ripe tomatoes, thickly sliced**

Add salt and pepper to corn meal. Dredge tomatoes in corn meal, coating both sides. Heat bacon grease in a heavy skillet and fry tomatoes until brown on both sides (turn only once).

Serves 3 to 4.

Vegetable Casserole

Helen Warren from Kinston (NC) makes this casserole and gets
raves. Try it, you'll see why.

1	can (16 ounce) French style green beans
1	can (12 ounces) shoe peg corn
1	can cream of celery soup
1/2	cup chopped onion
1/2	cup chopped celery
1/2	cup sour cream
1/2	teaspoon salt
1/2	teaspoon pepper
1/2	cup grated Cheddar cheese
1/2	stick butter or margarine
1	cup Ritz cracker crumbs
2	ounces almonds, sliced

Preheat oven to 350 degrees.

Mix beans, corn, celery soup, onion, celery, sour cream, salt, pepper, and cheese. Pour into a greased 1 1/2-quart casserole dish. Melt butter. Add cracker crumbs and almonds. Stir well until crumbs are coated. Place on top of casserole. Bake for 45 minutes.

Serves 6 to 8.

Fruits & Vegetables ••••••••••••••••••••••••••

_____

_____

_____

_____

_____

_____

_____

_____

_____

Beef

Beef............................

Beef Burgundy

This is an easy, inexpensive dish.

2	**pounds stew beef, cut into cubes**
1	**can (10 1/2 ounces) cream of mushroom soup**
1	**package dried onion soup mix**
1/2	**cup red wine**
1	**pound (8-10) medium sized fresh mushrooms**

Preheat oven to 300 degrees.

Combine beef, soup, soup mix, wine and mushrooms in a greased 1-quart casserole. Cover tightly and bake for 3 hours. Serve over rice or noodles.

Serves 6.

Beef Stew in Beer

This is always a treat for my family. Leftovers taste even better the next day.

2	pounds stew beef, cut into cubes
	all-purpose flour
3	tablespoons oil
1	medium onion, chopped
1	clove garlic
1	teaspoon salt
12	ounces beer
1	bay leaf
8 to 10	large fresh mushrooms, sliced
	carrots, cut into 1/2 inch slices
2	stalks celery, chopped
8	small new potatoes

Dredge meat in the flour. Heat the oil in a large skillet. Add the beef and cook until browned. Add onions, garlic and salt and saute for 2 to 3 minutes. Add beer and bay leaf. Cover and simmer for 1 1/2 hours or until meat is tender. Add mushrooms, carrots, celery, and potatoes and cook for 1/2 hour or until potatoes are tender.

Remove garlic clove and bay leaf and serve immediately.

Serves 4.

Beef Stroganoff

You can prepare this ahead and heat just before serving.

6	tablespoons butter
2	pounds filet or sirloin of beef, sliced into 1/2 inch strips
1	cup chopped onion
1	clove garlic, minced
1/2	pound fresh mushrooms
3	tablespoons all-purpose flour
2	bouillon cubes
1	tablespoon catsup
1/2	teaspoon salt
1/2	teaspoon pepper
1	can beef broth
1/4	cup dry white wine
1/4	teaspoon dried dill weed
1 1/2	cup sour cream

Melt butter in a large skillet. add beef and cook until brown. Remove the beef from the skillet and set aside. Add onions, garlic and mushrooms to the skillet and saute for 5 minutes. Add flour, bouillon cubes, catsup, salt, and pepper. Stir until smooth. Add broth and simmer for 5 minutes. Add wine, dill weed, and sour cream. Stir well, then add beef and simmer until hot. Serve over rice or noodles.

Serves 6.

Beef Wellington

This takes a little extra preparation, but it is well worth the effort!

---

4 to 6	pounds whole tenderloin of beef
1	clove garlic, halved
	salt and pepper to taste
6	strips bacon
	pastry (see below)
	filling (see next page)
1	egg, lightly beaten
	wine sauce (see next page)

Preheat oven to 450 degrees.

Rub the beef all over with the cut side of the garlic. Sprinkle beef with salt and pepper. Place bacon over the beef. Place beef in a roasting pan and bake for 45 minutes or until meat registers rare with a meat thermometer. While meat is cooking, prepare pastry and filling. Remove the meat from the oven and reduce heat to 425 degrees. Roll pastry out on a floured board until it is large enough to enclose the beef. Lay beef on one edge of pastry. Cover with the filling. Pull pastry over the meat, overlapping and sealing. Brush edges with beaten egg to seal. Place on a baking sheet, sealed edge down. Brush all over with egg. Bake about 30 minutes or until the pastry is cooked and lightly brown. Cut into thick slices and serve immediately with wine sauce.

Serves 10.

Pastry:

4	cups all-purpose flour
1	teaspoon salt
1/2	cup butter or margarine
1/2	cup shortening
1	egg, beaten

Place flour, salt, butter and shortening in a mixing bowl. Blend together until the mixture resembles large bread crumbs. Add egg and enough ice water to make the mixture form a ball. Wrap in wax paper and chill in the refrigerator until ready to use.

Beef Wellington (continued)

Don't dispair, you're almost there...

Filling:
1/4	cup butter or margarine
1/4	cup chopped onion
1/2	cup chopped mushrooms
1/4	cup cognac
1/2	pound ground veal
1/2	pound ground pork
1	egg beaten
1/4	cup heavy cream
1/4	cup chopped parsley
1	teaspoon salt
1/4	teaspoon basil
1/4	teaspoon thyme
1/4	teaspoon rosemary
1/8	teaspoon allspice
1/8	teaspoon pepper

Melt butter in a medium saucepan. Stir in onions, mushrooms and cognac. Cook over medium heat for 10 minutes. Pour mixture into a large bowl and add veal, pork, egg, cream, parsley, salt, basil, thyme, rosemary, allspice, and pepper. Mix lightly but thoroughly. Cover and refrigerate until ready to use.

Wine Sauce:
2	tablespoons butter or margarine
2	tablespoons finely chopped onion
1 1/2	cups canned beef gravy
2	tablespoons lemon juice
1/4	cup Madeira

Melt butter in a small saucepan. Add onion, gravy, and lemon juice. Bring to a boil. Stir in Madeira.

Beef Bake

Gather the crowd on Sunday night and enjoy this one.

1	pound ground beef (use ground chuck)
1/2	cup finely chopped green pepper
1/2	cup finely chopped onion
1/2	cup mayonnaise
1	teaspoon salt
1	egg, beaten
3/4	cup instant potato flakes
1/4	cup olive oil
3	slices processed American cheese
1	can (10 3/4 ounces) cream of celery soup
1/3	cup milk
3	English muffins, sliced and toasted

Preheat oven to 350 degrees.

Combine beef, green pepper, onion, mayonnaise, and salt. Shape into 6 patties. Combine egg and 1 tablespoon water. Dip patties into egg mixture, then coat with potato flakes. Brown lightly in hot oil . Arrange patties in a shallow baking dish. Cut cheese into 6 triangles and place one on each patty. Combine soup and milk and pour around the patties. Bake for 25 minutes. Serve on English muffins.

Serves 6.

Chili

This is great to serve on a cold day. Leftovers freeze well.

5	pounds ground beef (use ground chuck)
2	large onions, chopped
1	large green pepper, chopped
1/4	cup olive oil
3	large cans (16 ounces each) tomatoes
	salt and pepper to taste
3	tablespoons chili powder
1	teaspoon crushed red peppers
5	cans (10 ounces each) kidney beans

Saute beef, onion and green pepper in olive oil until meat is brown. Add tomatoes, salt, pepper, chili powder, and crushed red peppers. Cook over medium heat for about 1 hour. Add beans and cook for an additional 1/2 hour.

Serves 15.

Corned Beef

This is a touch of Germany, so serve with your favorite German white wine (who says you have to have a red wine with beef?).

1	corn beef brisket (3 pounds), trimmed
2	cloves garlic, minced
2	bay leaves
1/2	teaspoon salt
8	small new potatoes
4	medium carrots, scraped and quartered
4	medium onions, halved
1	medium head cabbage, cut into thin wedges

Place brisket in a Dutch oven. Add 4 cups of water, garlic, bay leaves, and salt. Bring to a boil. Cover, reduce heat, and simmer for 2 1/2 hours Add potatoes, carrots, and onions. Cover and cook for 10 minutes. Add cabbage. Cover and cook for 15 to 20 minutes or until cabbage is tender. Remove bay leaves.

Serves 6 to 8.

Moussaka

Serve with garlic toast.

2	pounds ground beef (use ground chuck)
2	cups sliced onion
	salt to taste
	garlic salt to taste
1 1/2	teaspoons all-purpose flour
1 1/2	teaspoons sugar
1	teaspoon basil
1 1/2	teaspoons cinnamon
1/4	teaspoon lemon pepper
1/4	teaspoon oregano
2	cans (8 ounces) tomato sauce
1	can (4 ounces) mushrooms
1	cup (8 ounces) shredded Swiss cheese
1	cup sour cream
4	cups thinly cut egg plant, parboiled 5 minutes and drained

Preheat oven to 350 degrees.

Brown meat in a skillet. Add onion, salt, and garlic salt and cook for 2 minutes. Stir in flour, sugar, basil, cinnamon, lemon pepper, and oregano. Mix well. Add tomato sauce and mushrooms and simmer for about 15 minutes. Combine cheese and sour cream in a bowl and set aside.

Grease a 2-quart casserole. Layer eggplant, meat mixture and cheese mixture. Bake for 35 minutes or until bubbly.

Serves 8 to 10.

Lasagna

For quick and easy preparation, use prepared spaghetti sauce and add 1 pound of browned and drained ground chuck.

3	cups ricotta cheese
3	cups shredded mozzarella cheese
2	eggs
6	cups of spaghetti sauce
12	cooked lasagna noodles
1/2	cup grated parmesan cheese

Preheat oven to 400 degrees.

Mix ricotta cheese, mozzarella cheese and eggs. Grease 2 2-quart shallow baking dishes. Layer 1 cup spaghetti sauce, 2 noodles, 1 cup cheese mixture. Repeat layers. Top with remaining noodles, sauce and Parmesan cheese. Bake for 30 minutes or until brown and bubbly. This freezes well too!

Serves 8 to 10.

Baked Liver and Onions

For those who like beef liver, this is for you.

2	large onions, cut into 1/2 inch slices
1/2	cup butter or margarine
1/2	cup dry red wine
1/4	cup chopped parsley
1	bay leaf, crumbled
1	teaspoon thyme
	salt and freshly ground pepper to taste
6	slices of beef liver
1/2	cup all-purpose flour

Preheat oven to 350 degrees.

Arrange onions in a shallow baking dish. Dot with butter. Add wine, parsley, bay leaf, thyme, salt, pepper, and 1/2 cup water. Cover and bake for 30 minutes. Coat liver in flour. Place on top of onion slices. Cover and bake for 30 minutes, basting 2 or 3 times. Remove cover and continue cooking for 10 more minutes.

Serves 6.

Stuffed Manicotti

Combine with your favorite salad and bread, then top off with red wine, and you've got a great meal for 2.

4	manicotti shells
	salt to taste
1/2	pound ground chuck
1	small onion, finely chopped
1/2	green pepper, finely chopped
1	can (15 ounces) tomato sauce
1/2	teaspoon garlic powder
2	teaspoons oregano
1	teaspoon thyme
1	bay leaf
1	cup shredded mozzarella cheese, divided

Preheat oven to 300 degrees.

Cook manicotti in 3 quarts of boiling, salted water for 10 minutes. Drain, rinse, drain, and set aside. Saute beef, onion, and green pepper until brown. Drain off the excess grease. Add tomato sauce, garlic powder, oregano, thyme, and bay leaf. Simmer over low heat for 10 minutes. Add 1/2 cup of the cheese, stirring until the cheese is melted.

Arrange the manicotti shells in a greased shallow baking dish. Stuff with half of the meat mixture. Pour remaining meat mixture over the shells and sprinkle remaining cheese over the shells. Bake for 30 minutes.

Serves 2.

Macaroni and Beef

Before there was Hamburger Helper, we made this the "old fashioned way."

1 1/2	pounds ground chuck
1	medium onion, diced
1	can (28 ounces) tomatoes
1	package (8 ounces) elbow macaroni
2	cups shredded Cheddar cheese
1	jar (2 ounces) pimento-stuffed olives, drained and sliced
1	teaspoon salt
1/4	teaspoon pepper

Saute beef and onion in a skillet over medium heat about 10 minutes or until brown, stirring frequently. Stir in tomatoes (with liquid), 1 cup of water, macaroni, cheese, olives, salt and pepper. Heat to boiling. Reduce heat to low. Cover and simmer for 25 minutes or until macaroni is tender.

Serves 6.

Meat Loaf

Serve with escalloped potatoes and you have a quick, but easy, meal.

2	**pounds ground chuck**
2	**eggs**
1 1/2	**cups bread crumbs**
3/4	**cup catsup**
1	**teaspoon Accent (optional)**
1	**package dried onion soup mix**
3	**strips bacon**
1	**can (8 ounces) tomato sauce**

Preheat oven to 350 degrees.

Combine beef, eggs, bread crumbs, catsup, Accent, 1/2 cup warm water and soup mix. Place mixture into a greased loaf pan. Cover with bacon strips and pour tomato sauce over top. Bake for 1 hour.

Serves 6.

Pot Roast

Leftovers are great the next day.

2	tablespoons olive oil
4	pounds chuck, rump, or round roast
1	can (10 3/4 ounces) cream of mushroom soup
1	package dried onion soup mix
6	medium potatoes, quartered
6	carrots, cut into 2 inch pieces
1	cup diced celery
15	small whole fresh mushrooms
2	tablespoons all-purpose flour
	chopped fresh parsley

Heat oil in a 6-quart pot over medium heat. Add meat and brown on all sides. Pour off excess fat. Stir in mushroom soup, onion soup mix and 1 cup of water. Reduce heat to low. Cover and cook for 2 hours. Add potatoes, carrots, celery, and mushrooms. Cover and cook for 45 minutes or until roast and vegetables are tender.

Remove roast and vegetables from the pot. Combine flour and 1/4 cup water, stirring until smooth. Gradually add to soup mixture in the pot. Cook mixture until it boils and thickens, stirring constantly. Serve over the meat and vegetables. Garnish with parsley.

Serves 6.

Sloppy Joes

For children of all ages...

1 1/2	pounds ground chuck
1	large onion, chopped
2	cloves garlic, chopped
1	green pepper, chopped
1	can (15 ounces) tomato sauce
1	teaspoon thyme
1/4	cup catsup
2	teaspoons Worchestershire sauce
	hot pepper sauce to taste
	salt and pepper to taste
8	hard rolls or hamburger buns (split, lightly toasted and buttered)

Brown chuck with the onions, garlic and green pepper in a large skillet over medium heat for about 10 minutes. Pour off excess fat. Add tomato sauce, 1/2 cup water, and thyme. Reduce heat and simmer, uncovered, for 10 minutes. Stir in catsup, Worchestershire sauce, and hot sauce. Simmer for 5 more minutes, stirring frequently, until the mixture thickens (add a little water if mixture becomes too thick). Spoon onto bottom half of each roll.

Makes 8 servings.

Spaghetti Sauce

This sauce is great to fix today, divide up and freeze for later.
You can also use this sauce as the base for lasagna.

2	pounds ground chuck
1	large onion, chopped
1	green pepper, chopped
1	cup diced celery
2	cans (8 ounces) tomato sauce
1	can (16 ounces) tomatoes, chopped (retain liquid)
1	pound (8-10 large) fresh mushrooms, sliced
1	teaspoon garlic salt
1	teaspoon crushed red peppers
2	teaspoons oregano
	salt and pepper to taste
	very thin spaghetti noodles, cooked
	grated Parmesan cheese

Saute beef, onion, green pepper, and celery until beef is brown. Drain off excess grease. Add tomato sauce, tomatoes and liquid, mushrooms, garlic salt, red peppers, oregano, salt and pepper. Cover and simmer for 3 hours, stirring occasionally. Serve over cooked, very thin spaghetti noodles topped with grated Parmesan cheese.

Serves 6.

Spaghetti Bake

Prepare ahead and bake when you're ready.

2	slices bacon
2	medium onions, chopped
1	clove garlic, minced
1/2	pound ground chuck
	salt and pepper to taste
1	teaspoon oregano
1/2	teaspoon marjoram
1/2	teaspoon sugar
2	cans (8 ounces) tomato sauce
1/2	pound uncooked very thin spaghetti
1	cup grated Cheddar cheese
1/4	cup grated Parmesan cheese

Preheat oven to 350 degrees.

Fry bacon in a large skillet for 2 minutes. Place bacon on a paper towel to cool, then chop into pieces. Add onions, garlic and beef to the skillet and saute until brown. Drain excess grease. Stir in salt and pepper, oregano, marjoram, sugar, bacon pieces, tomato sauce, and 2 1/2 cups water. Cover and simmer 25 minutes.

Break half of the noodles into a greased 2-quart casserole. Cover with half of the sauce and half of the Cheddar cheese. Repeat layers. Top wth Parmesan cheese. Cover and bake for 30 minutes or until casserole is bubbly and noodles are tender.

Serves 4 to 6.

Spanish Rice

Children love this. Serve it with a salad or vegetable and you have a meal!

4	strips bacon
1	large onion, chopped
1	green pepper, chopped
1	pound ground chuck
1	can (16 ounces) tomatoes
1/2	cup uncooked rice
	salt and pepper to taste

Fry bacon, remove from pan and drain on a paper towel. Saute onion and green pepper in the bacon drippings. Add beef and saute until beef is browned. Drain excess grease. Add tomatoes, rice, salt and pepper. Crumble bacon and add to mixture. Cover and simmer over low heat for 30 minutes or until rice is done. If mixture becomes too thick before rice is done, add a little water.

Serves 4.

Stuffed Peppers

These freeze well.

6	**green peppers**
1	**pound ground chuck**
1/2	**cup cooked, fluffy rice**
1	**cup chopped onion**
1	**clove garlic, minced**
1	**teaspoon basil**
1	**tablespoon lemon juice**
	salt and pepper to taste
3	**cans (8 ounces) tomato sauce**

Preheat oven to 350 degrees.

Slice tops off peppers and remove the seeds. Wash and set aside.

Brown beef in a skillet. Pour off excess grease. Place beef in a large bowl and mash with a fork. Add rice, onions, garlic, basil, lemon juice, salt and pepper. Mix well. Add 1 cup tomato sauce and mix well. Pack mixture into pepper casing and arrange in a greased casserole dish. Pour remaining tomato sauce over peppers and sprinkle with salt and pepper. Bake uncovered for 30 minutes or until tender.

Serves 6.

Sukiyaki

Serve with egg rolls and you've got a winner.

2	ounces beef suet, cut up
2	onions, sliced thin
1	cup chopped celery
2	cups sliced fresh mushrooms
1	pound fresh spinach, cut into 1 inch strips
6	scallions, cut up
2	cups bean sprouts
2	pounds round steak, sliced thin
1/4	cup soy sauce
1/2	cup beef broth
1	teaspoon sugar
	salt and pepper to taste
	cooked white rice

Fry suet in a large skillet or wok. Add onions and celery and saute for 2 to 3 minutes. Remove suet. Add mushrooms, spinach, scallions, and bean sprouts. Cook at high heat for 5 minutes. Push vegetables to one side. Add beef and fry for 3 minutes. Stir beef and vegetables together. Add soy sauce, broth, sugar, salt and pepper. Cook 5 minutes, stirring frequently. Serve over rice.

Serves 6.

Beef •••••••••••••••••••••••••••••••••••

_____

_____

_____

_____

_____

_____

_____

_____

_____

Pork

Pork •

Pork Chops and Apples

A perfect combination.

2	tablespoons butter or margarine
4	pork loin chops, 1 inch thick
1	cup chopped Granny Smith apples
1/4	cup firmly packed brown sugar
1/2	teaspoon cinnamon
4	lemon slices

Melt butter in a large skillet over medium heat. Add pork chops and brown, about 2 minutes on each side. Place 1/4 cup apples on top of each pork chop. Reduce heat to low and cook covered for 20 minutes or until apples are tender. Mix brown sugar and cinnamon. Sprinkle over chops. Top each chop with a lemon slice. Cover skillet again. Cook 5 minutes longer or until sugar is melted.

Serves 4.

Pork Chop and Cabbage

Serve with fruit salad.

4	pork chops, 3/4 inch thick
1	tablespoon cooking oil
1	medium onion, sliced
1/2	cup dry white wine
1/4	cup packed brown sugar
1	tablespoon white wine vinegar
1	teaspoon salt
1/4	teaspoon pepper
4	cups shredded cabbage
2	large cooking apples, cored and thinly sliced

Preheat oven to 350 degrees.

Place oil in a large ovenproof skillet over medium heat. Place pork chops in the skillet and brown on both sides. Remove chops from skillet and set aside. Add onion and cook until tender. Stir in wine, brown sugar, vinegar, salt and pepper. Stir in cabbage and apples. Bring mixture to a boil and top with pork chops. Cover and bake for 40 to 45 minutes or until pork chops are tender.

Serves 4.

Creole Pork Chops

Serve with a medley of vegetables.

4	center-cut loin pork chops
	salt and pepper to taste
1	cup uncooked rice
2	medium size green peppers, chopped
2	medium onions, chopped
1/4	cup catsup

Season pork chops with salt and pepper and place in a large skillet. Cover with rice, green pepper, and onion. Add additional salt and pepper. Combine 2 1/2 cups boiling water and catsup and pour over the pork chops. Bring to a boil. Cover, lower heat and simmer for 1 hour or until rice is tender.

Serves 4.

Baked Stuffed Pork Chops

Try serving hot slaw with this.

6	pork chops, cut 1 1/4 to 1 1/2 inch thick with a pocket salt and pepper to taste
1 1/2	cups toasted bread cubes
1/2	cup chopped apple
1/2	cup shredded sharp Cheddar cheese
2	tablespoons light raisins
2	tablespoons butter or margarine, melted
2	tablespoons orange juice
1/8	teaspoon ground cinnamon

Preheat oven to 350 degrees.

Sprinkle inside of pork with salt and pepper. Combine bread cubes, apple, cheese. raisins, butter, orange juice, salt and cinnamon. Toss gently and stuff into the pocket of each pork chop. Place in a shallow baking dish and bake for 1 1/4 hours. Cover with foil and bake 15 more minutes.

Serves 6.

Pork Chop and Potato Casserole

This one was another favorite of Aunt Jess Heller's from New Milford (CT). Great served with German red cabbage.

1	tablespoon salad oil
4	loin pork chops, 1 inch thick
4	medium potatoes
1	small onion
3	tablespoons all-purpose flour
	salt and pepper to taste
1/2	stick butter or margarine
1	cup milk
1	can (10 3/4 ounce) cream of mushroom or cream of celery soup

Preheat oven to 325 degrees.

Heat oil in a large skillet. Add pork chops and brown on both sides. Set aside. Peel and cut potatoes into thin slices. Peel and cut onions in thin slices. In a greased 2-quart casserole, place a layer of potatoes and onion. Sprinkle layer with flour, salt and pepper. Dot with butter. Continue layers until all ingredients are used. Pour in milk. Bake in oven for 15 minutes.

Remove casserole from oven and add pork chops to top. Pour soup over pork chops. Cover and return to the oven to bake for 45 minutes or until chops and potatoes are done.

Serves 4.

Pork Chop and 'Kraut Casserole

Try pork with a German touch.

4	**loin pork chops, 1 inch thick**
1	**tablespoon vegetable oil**
1	**can (10 ounces) sauerkraut**
1	**medium onion, sliced**
	salt and pepper to taste
1	**can (10 3/4 ounces) condensed tomato soup**

Preheat oven to 350 degrees.

Heat oil in a large skillet. Put the chops in the skillet and brown on both sides. In a greased 1 1/2-quart casserole, layer sauerkraut, pork chops, and onion. Add salt and pepper. Pour soup over all ingredients. Cover and bake for 1 hour.

Serves 4.

Sausage and Rice Casserole

Alice Wheatly from Beaufort (NC) shared this. Serve for lunch, brunch or supper.

1 1/2	pounds hot sausage
1	large green pepper, chopped
1	large onion, chopped
1	cup diced celery
1/2	cup rice
2	envelopes chicken noodle soup mix
1	package slivered almonds
	paprika
	chopped parsley

Preheat oven to 350 degrees.

Brown and drain sausage. Saute pepper, onion, and celery. Boil 4 1/2 cups water and add rice and soup mix. Cook 7 minutes and combine sausage, vegetables, and soup in a greased 1 1/2-quart casserole. Sprinkle top with almonds, paprika, and parsley. Bake for 30 minutes or until rice is cooked.

Serves 4 to 6.

Smoked Sausage and Macaroni

Just add your favorite salad ...

2	tablespoons butter or margarine
1	pound smoked sausage, cut into 1/4 inch slices
1	medium onion, chopped
1/2	cup chopped green pepper
1/2	cup sliced celery
4	cups cooked elbow macaroni
2	cans (8 ounce) tomato sauce
1	teaspoon chili powder
1/4	teaspoon pepper
1/2	cup (2 ounces) shredded sharp Cheddar cheese

Melt butter in a large skillet. Add sausage, onion, green pepper, and celery. Saute until vegetables are tender. Stir in macaroni, tomato sauce, chili powder, and pepper. Cook over low heat, stirring frequently, until thouroughly heated. Sprinkle with cheese and continue cooking until cheese melts.

Serves 4.

Baked Barbecue Pork Ribs

Try the cranberry-apple casserole as a side dish.

5	pounds (2 strips) fresh pork spare ribs, fat trimmed
1	cup bottled barbecue sauce (or use Barbecue Sauce II recipe)
2	tablespoons wine vinegar
3	cloves garlic
1/4	cup soy sauce
1/4	teaspoon dry mustard
2	tablespoons red wine
2	tablespoons sugar
1/4	teaspoon ground ginger

Score meat with a sharp knife but don't cut all the way through. Place ribs in a shallow roasting pan large enough to let them lie flat.

Combine barbecue sauce, vinegar, garlic, soy sauce, mustard, wine, sugar and ginger in a small bowl and pour over the meat. Cover and refrigerate at least 1 hour, turning occasionally.

Preheat oven to 350 degrees.

Drain marinade into a small bowl and set aside. Bake meat in the oven for 1 hour and 45 minutes, basting occasionally with marinade. Just prior to serving, place meat under a preheated broiler for about 5 minutes, until meat is crisp.

Serves 8 to 10.

Pork Tenderloin

You can also slice and use as an hors d'oeuvre with hot rolls.

---

2   pork tenderloins (1 to 1 1/2 pounds each)

Marinade:
1   cup soy sauce
1/4   cup sesame seeds
5   tablespoons sugar
3   tablespoons minced onion
2   tablespoons ground ginger
1   tablespoon garlic powder

Place pork in a shallow roasting pan. Mix soy sauce, sesame seeds, sugar, onion, ginger, and garlic powder and pour over the pork. Cover and refrigerate for at least 3 hours, turning occasionally.

Preheat oven to 375 degrees.

Bake for 45 minutes or until pork is done.

Serves 6 to 8.

Pork Marsala

The wine makes the difference with this one.

1	**pound pork tenderloin**
1	**tablespoon oil**
1	**tablespoon butter or margarine**
1	**clove garlic, minced**
1	**tablespoon tomato paste**
1/2	**cup Marsala wine**
8	**ounces fresh mushrooms**
1	**teaspoon chopped parsley**

Cut tenderloin diagonally into cutlets. Pound to 1/4" thickness. Heat oil and butter in a heavy skillet. Brown cutlets on both sides. Remove from pan and set aside. Add garlic to pan and saute. Mix in tomato sauce and wine. Add mushrooms. Stir to blend with pan juices. Simmer 3 to 5 minutes. Return cutlets to the pan and heat thoroughly. Sprinkle with parsley and serve immediately.

Serves 4.

Pork Roast

This is well worth the extra effort.

---

5   pounds boneless rolled pork loin roast
2   teaspoons cornstarch

Marinade:
1/2   cup dry red wine
1/4   cup packed brown sugar
3   tablespoons vinegar
3   tablespoons catsup
1   tablespoon cooking oil
1   tablespoon soy sauce
1   clove garlic, minced
1   teaspoon curry powder
1/4   teaspoon ground ginger
1/4   teaspoon pepper

Untie the rolled roast to trim fat. Reroll roast and tie with a kitchen string. Place meat into a plastic bag and place in a shallow dish.

Prepare marinade by combining wine, sugar, 3 tablespoons water, vinegar, catsup, oil, soy sauce, garlic, curry powder, ginger, and pepper. Pour marinade into the plastic bag with the meat. Close bag and place meat in the refrigerator for 6 to 8 hours, turning several times to distribute the marinade. Drain meat, reserving 1 cup.

Preheat oven to 325 degrees.

Pat meat dry and place on a rack in a shallow roasting pan. Bake for 2 hours or until meat thermometer registers 160 degrees. Meanwhile, combine 1/4 cup cold water and cornstarch in a small saucepan. Add reserved marinade. Cook and stir until mixture is thickened and bubbly. Cook and stir 1 to 2 minutes more. Brush meat with marinade. Continue roasting 1 hour more or until thermometer registers 170 degrees, brushing meat frequently. Spoon remaining marinade over meat before serving.

Serves 8 to 10.

Pork ●

_____

_____

_____

_____

_____

_____

_____

_____

Poultry

Artichoke Chicken

An easy way to make chicken a special dish.

2	large chicken breasts, boned, skinned, and halved
1/4	cup all-purpose flour
1/2	stick butter or margarine
8 to 10	fresh mushrooms, sliced
1	can (15 ounces) artichoke hearts, rinsed and well drained
1/2	cup chicken stock or broth
1/4	cup white wine
	juice of 1/2 lemon or to taste
	salt and pepper to taste

Dredge chicken with flour, shake off excess. Melt butter in medium skillet, add chicken, and saute until golden brown and cooked. Transfer chicken to a heated platter. Add mushrooms to the skillet and saute 1 to 2 minutes. Stir in artichoke hearts, stock, wine, lemon juice, salt and pepper. Let cook until sauce is slightly reduced, stirring occasionally.

Return chicken to the skillet and warm through. Serve immediately.

Makes 4 servings.

Chicken with Asparagus

This is great to serve to the bridge club.

2	breasts of chicken, cut in half and boned
1 1/2	teaspoons Accent (optional)
1/4	teaspoon pepper
1/2	cup corn oil
2	packages (10 ounces each) frozen asparagus, cooked and drained
1	can (10 3/4 ounces) cream of chicken, celery or mushroom soup, undiluted
1/2	cup mayonnaise
1	tablespoon lemon juice
1	teaspoon curry powder
1	cup shredded sharp Cheddar cheese

Preheat oven to 375 degrees.

Sprinkle Accent and pepper over chicken. Heat oil in a skillet and saute chicken about 10 minutes over medium heat. Remove chicken and drain on a paper towel. Place asparagus in a greased 9" x 9" x 2" baking dish. Put chicken on top of asparagus. Combine soup, mayonnaise, lemon juice, and curry powder. Pour over the chicken. Sprinkle cheese on top. Bake for 30 minutes or until bubbly.

Serves 4.

Chicken Bake

Joyce Benner from Raleigh (NC) served this easy recipe that enticed my finicky daughter, Jess, to eat 3 servings!

3	cups cooked, diced chicken
1	can (10 3/4 ounces) cream of chicken soup
1	cup diced celery
2	tablespoons minced onion
1	tablespoon chopped fresh parsley
1/2	teaspoon salt
1/4	teaspoon pepper
1	tablespoon lemon juice
3/4	cup mayonnaise
3	hard boiled eggs, chopped
1/3	cup slivered almonds
1	cup shredded sharp Cheddar cheese
	sherry to taste
2	cups crushed potato chips

Preheat oven to 400 degrees.

Combine chicken, soup, celery, onion, parsley, salt, pepper, lemon juice, mayonnaise, eggs, almonds, cheese and sherry in a greased 2-quart casserole. Top with potato chips. Bake for 20 minutes or until bubbly.

Serves 4 to 6.

Chicken Breasts in Cream Sauce

This dish can be prepared ahead or served immediately. You may want to add 1/2 cup white wine with the chicken broth.

6	large chicken breasts, boned and cut in half
2	cans (13 3/4) chicken broth
1/2	cup chopped celery
1/2	cup chopped onion
1	cup chopped carrots
2	teaspoons salt

Sauce:

3	tablespoons butter or margarine
1/4	cup diced green pepper
3	tablespoons all-purpose flour
2	cups light cream or half and half
1/2	teaspoon salt
1/4	teaspoon curry
2	tablespoons diced pimento

Place chicken in a Dutch oven. Add broth, celery, onion, carrots, and salt. Cover and simmer gently until chicken is tender, about 1 1/4 hours. Remove breasts. Place broth and vegetables from the Dutch oven into a blender and puree.

To make the sauce, melt butter in a large saucepan. Add green pepper and saute lightly. Blend in flour. Add 1 1/2 cups of the vegetable puree and cream, stirring until smooth and thickened. Add salt and curry. Stir in pimento and simmer 5 minutes.

Arrange chicken in a shallow pan. Pour sauce over the chicken. Chicken may be frozen for later use or placed in the oven and baked until heated through and bubbly, about 10 minutes.

Serves 6 to 8.

Barbecued Cranberry Chicken

This has a real tangy flavor.

2   broiler-fryer chickens (about 3 pounds each), quartered
        salt and pepper to taste

Barbecue sauce:
1   can (16 ounces) whole berry cranberry sauce
1   cup chili sauce
1/2   cup chicken broth or 1 bouillon cube
        juice of 1 lemon
1   tablespoon Worchestershire sauce
1   tablespoon minced onion
1   teaspoon dry mustard

Sprinkle chicken on all sides with salt and pepper. Combine cranberry sauce, chili sauce, broth, lemon juice, Worchestershire sauce, onion, and mustard in a blender. Blend until smooth.

Place chicken 8 inches above gray coals and grill for 30 minutes, turning every 10 minutes. Brush chicken with barbecue sauce and continue grilling for another 20 minutes, brushing with the barbecue sauce every 10 minutes.

Serves 6 to 8.

Barbecued Lemon Chicken

This marinade makes plain grilled chicken become special.

2	**tablespoons butter or margarine**
1	**garlic clove, minced**
1	**can (8 ounces) tomato sauce**
1/2	**cup Worchestershire sauce**
2	**tablespoons lemon juice**
1/2	**teaspoon salt**
2 1/2	**pounds chicken, cut into pieces**

Melt butter in a medium saucepan. Add garlic and saute for 1 minute. Blend in tomato sauce, Worchestershire sauce, lemon juice and salt. Bring to a boil, then reduce heat. Simmer, uncovered, for 5 minutes. Remove from heat and cool. Place chicken in a shallow baking dish. Pour half of the sauce over the chicken. Turn chicken so that both sides are coated. Cover and refrigerate for 24 hours. Refrigerate the remaining sauce.

Grill or broil for 25-30 minutes on each side or until chicken is done. Brush with remaining sauce while cooking.

Makes 6 servings.

Marinated Barbecued Chicken

This tastes great served with broiled tomatoes, onions, and other
vegetables.

2   broiler-fryer chickens (about 2 1/2 pounds each), cut up

Marinade:
1/2	teaspoon grated lemon peel	1/4	teaspoon pepper
1/4	cup lemon juice	1/8	teaspoon leaf
1/3	cup olive oil		oregano, crushed
1	small clove garlic, finely chopped		

Barbecue sauce:
2   tablespoons unsalted butter or margarine
1   medium onion, chopped
1   clove garlic, finely chopped
1   teaspoon chopped fresh ginger
1   cup chili sauce
1   bottle (10 ounces) ginger ale
1   tablespoon Worchestershire sauce
2   tablespoons cider vinegar
2   cans (8 ounces each) tomato sauce

Place chicken in a large shallow glass dish. Prepare marinade
by combining lemon peel and juice in a small bowl. Slowly blend in oil,
garlic, pepper, and oregano. Pour over the chicken. Cover and
refrigerate at least 1 hour, turning chicken several times.

Meanwhile, prepare the barbecue sauce by melting butter in a
large saucepan over medium heat. Add onion and saute 1 minute. Add
garlic and ginger and cook for 5 minutes, continually stirring. Add chili
sauce, tomato sauce, ginger ale, Worchestershire sauce, and vinegar.
Bring to a boil, then lower heat and simmer for about 40 minutes. Set
aside 2 cups for serving with chicken. Use remaining to cook chicken.

Remove chicken from marinade, reserve marinade. Broil
chicken 6 to 8 inches from heat, basting with marinade, until meat is no
longer pink, about 20 mintes per side. Brush one side with barbecue
sauce. Broil until crisp, about 4 minutes. Turn chicken and repeat.

Serves 6 to 8.

Chicken and Broccoli Casserole

This is a great luncheon dish served with frozen fruit salad.

1	can (10 3/4 ounces) cream of mushroom soup
1	cup mayonnaise
1	teaspoon curry powder
1	teaspoon Worchestershire sauce
2	tablespoons lemon juice
	dash of red pepper
1/4	teaspoon salt
3	cups cooked, diced chicken
1	package (10 ounces) frozen broccoli, partially cooked and drained
2	cups buttered bread crumbs
3	tablespoons slivered almonds

Preheat oven to 350 degrees.

Make a sauce by combining soup, mayonnaise, curry powder, Worchestershire sauce, lemon juice, red pepper, and salt. Layer half of chicken and broccoli in a greased 2-quart baking dish. Pour half of the sauce over the mixture. Repeat layers and cover with remaining sauce. Sprinkle with bread crumbs, then with almonds. Bake for 30 minutes.

Makes 6 servings.

Brunswick Stew

Freezes well - if you have any leftovers.

1	broiler-fryer chicken (2 1/2 to 3 pounds)
1 1/2	pounds, lean beef for stewing, cut into 1-inch cubes
1	pound pork tenderloin
1	small head cabbage, cored and chopped
3	cans (16 ounces) tomatoes, undrained and chopped
6	medium potatoes, peeled and cubed
4	cups frozen butter beans
1	package (16 ounces) frozen white shoepeg corn
4	cups chopped onion
1	can (6 ounces) tomato paste
3	tablespoons Worchestershire sauce
2	tablespoons lemon juice
1	tablespoon sugar
2	teaspoons salt
1	teaspoon pepper

Place chicken in a Dutch oven and cover with water. Bring to a boil. Reduce heat, cover and simmer for 1 hour. Remove chicken from broth, reserving broth. Let chicken cool, then remove bone and coarsely chop the meat. Set aside.

Meanwhile, place beef and pork in a Dutch oven and cover with water. Bring to a boil. Reduce heat, cover and simmer for 2 hours. Remove meat from broth, reserving broth. Let meat cool and coarsely chop the meat. Set aside.

Combine chicken broth and beef and pork broth. Measure 6 to 7 cups of broth and combine with the meat in a large Dutch oven. Add cabbage, tomatoes, potatoes, beans, corn, onions, and tomato paste. Bring to a boil. Reduce heat, cover and simmer for 2 hours. Add Worchestershire sauce, lemon juice, sugar, salt and pepper. Mix well.

Makes about 2 gallons.

Chicken Cacciatore

Serve over cooked spaghetti with red wine.

2	pounds chicken pieces, deboned and cut into chunks
3	tablespoons self-rising flour
2	tablespoons olive oil
1	can (10 3/4 ounces) tomato soup
1/2	cup dry white wine
1/2	cup chopped onion
1	cup (about 1/4 pound) sliced fresh mushrooms
1/2	teaspoon basil leaves, crushed
1/2	teaspoon oregano leaves, crushed
2	large cloves garlic, minced
1	small bay leaf
1	small green pepper, cut in strips

Dust chicken in flour. Brown chicken in oil in a skillet. Add soup, wine, onion, mushrooms basil and oregano leaves, garlic, and bay leaf. Cover and cook over low heat for 30 minutes. Add green pepper. Cook 15 minutes more or until done, stirring occasionally. Remove bay leaf.

Serves 4.

Chinese Chicken Stirfry

Try this with Chinese fried rice for a complete meal.

4	chicken breasts
1	tablespoon cornstarch
3	tablespoons water
1	tablespoon sherry
1	teaspoon salt
1	green onion, chopped
1/4	teaspoon ground ginger
4	tablespoons peanut oil
1/4	pound blanched almonds
1/4	pound fresh mushrooms, cleaned and sliced
1	can sliced water chestnuts, drained
1	can bamboo shoots, drained
1/4	cup green beans (fresh, frozen or canned)
	soy sauce to taste

Cut chicken from bone in thin slices. Combine cornstarch and water. Add chicken, sherry, salt, onions, and ginger.

Heat oil in a skillet and fry almonds for 1 minute. Drain on a paper towel and set aside. Heat 1 tablespoon oil in the same skillet. Add mushrooms, water chestnuts, bamboo shoots and green beans. Saute for about 1 minute. Remove from pan and set aside. Heat remaining 2 tablespoons oil in the same skillet. Add chicken mixture and cook, stirring constantly, until chicken loses its raw look. Mix in vegetables and 1/2 of almonds. Continue stirring until mixture is heated through and chicken is done.

Garnish with the remaining almonds and serve with soy sauce.

Serves 4.

Chicken Breasts with Dried Beef

This is great served with wild rice.

4	boneless, skinless chicken breasts, cut in half
8	strips bacon
1	jar (5 ounces) dried beef
1/2	pint sour cream
1	can (10 3/4 ounces) mushroom soup
1/2	can (6 ounces) evaporated milk

Sauce:

2	tablespoons butter or margarine
6-8	fresh mushrooms, sliced
1	can (10 3/4 ounces) mushroom soup
1/4	cup sherry

Preheat oven to 350 degrees.

Line a greased 9" x 9" baking dish with 2 layers of dried beef. Wrap each half of chicken in a piece of bacon. Place in baking dish. Blend sour cream, soup and milk and pour over the chicken. DO NOT ADD SALT. Bake for about 1 1/2 hours or until chicken is done.

Melt butter in a skillet and add mushrooms. Saute until done. Add soup and sherry, stirring until blended. Arrange chicken on a platter and pour sauce over the chicken.

Serves 6 to 8.

22

Chicken Croquettes

These were a specialty of Chef Aver Lee Simmons at the Kinston Country Club and high on the request list of both my daughters.

2	tablespoons butter or margarine, melted			salt and pepper
3	tablespoons self-rising flour	10		slices "day old" white bread
1	cup chicken broth	2		eggs, beaten
2	cups cooked, chopped chicken			peanut oil
1	rib celery, chopped			

Sauce:

1/2	stick butter or margarine
8-10	medium size fresh mushrooms, cleaned and sliced
1	can (10 3/4 ounces) cream of mushroom soup
1	cup sherry
1	tablespoon lemon juice
1/2	cup slivered, toasted almonds

Make a white sauce by combining butter, flour and broth in a medium saucepan over low heat. Stir until slightly thickened. Add chicken, celery, salt and pepper and set aside to cool.

Remove crusts from bread and cut bread into small cubes (about 1/2 inch). Shape chicken mixture into croquettes (the shape and size of a large egg). Roll croquettes in egg and then in bread cubes. Place on a tray covered with wax paper. Cover and refrigerate for at least 2 hours or until ready to serve. (Croquettes may be frozen at this point, if desired, to use at a later date.)

Just before ready to serve, deep fry in peanut oil (heated to 350 degrees) until brown. Drain on paper towels until ready to serve.

While croquettes are frying, melt butter in a medium skillet. Add mushrooms. Saute until mushrooms are soft. Stir in mushroom soup, sherry and lemon juice. Heat thoroughly. Pour sauce over the croquettes and top with almonds.

Serves 6.

Crunchy Chicken Casserole

Prepare ahead so you can have time to enjoy your dinner guests.

1/2	pint sour cream
4	tablespoons bottled barbecue sauce
1	teaspoon lemon juice
2	teaspoons Worchestershire sauce
1	teaspoon celery salt
1	teaspoon paprika
1/2	teaspoon garlic salt
1/2	teaspoon pepper
8	chicken breasts, deboned and halved
	Escort crackers
	herb dressing mix
1/2	cup butter or margarine, melted

Combine sour cream, 2 tablespoons barbecue sauce, lemon juice, Worchestershire sauce, celery salt, paprika, garlic salt and pepper. Mix well. Add the chicken to the mixture and marinate overnight in a covered container.

Next day, 1 1/2 hours before serving, preheat oven to 350 degrees.

Roll the breasts in a meal made from the crackers and dressing mix. Place in a greased 2-quart baking dish. Pour butter combined with 2 tablespoons of barbecue sauce over the chicken. Cover and bake for 1 to 1 1/2 hours.

Serves 8.

Chicken Curry

Serve over rice. Place condiments in separate containers on a serving tray. Shrimp or lamb may be substituted for the hen.

1	whole chicken (4 to 5 pounds)
	salt and pepper to taste
1/2	cup chopped onion
1/2	cup chopped celery
1/4	cup butter or margarine
1/3	cup self-rising flour
2	cups chicken stock or broth
1	cup tomato juice
1/2	teaspoon Worchestershire sauce
1	teaspoon curry powder

Condiments:
almonds
chopped crisp bacon
coconut
chutney
finely chopped hard boiled eggs

Place hen in a large pan. Add salt and pepper and cover hen with water. Boil until done. Remove chicken from broth, reserving broth. Cool and remove bone.

Saute onion and celery in butter. Add flour and stock, stirring until thick. Add tomato juice, Worchestershire sauce, and curry powder. Add chicken. Cook until bubbling.

Serves 8.

Chicken and Dressing Casserole

This is another easy casserole that you can make ahead of time so you're not "stuck" in the kitchen when entertaining guests.

4	large chicken breasts
1	can (10 3/4 ounces) cream of chicken soup, undiluted
1	can (10 3/4 ounces) cream of mushroom soup, undiluted
1	package (8 ounces) herb-seasoned stuffing mix
1/2	cup butter or margarine, melted

Cook chicken in boiling water until tender. Remove chicken from broth. Strain broth, reserving 2 2/3 cups. Bone and dice chicken. Set aside. Combine chicken soup with half of the reserved broth. Mix well and set aside. Combine mushroom soup with remaining broth. Mix well and set aside.

Combine stuffing and butter, reserving 1/4 cup for topping. Spoon half of stuffing mixture in a greased 13" x 9" x 2" baking dish. Top with 1/2 of the chicken. Cover with the chicken soup mixture. Repeat layers. Top with mushroom soup mixture. Sprinkle with reserved stuffing mixture. Cover and refrigerate overnight.

Remove casserole from the refrigerator 15 minutes before baking. Preheat oven to 350 degrees. Uncover casserole and bake for 30 to 45 minutes.

Serves 8.

Hungarian Baked Chicken

This will make you think you are in Germany...

1/2	stick butter or margarine
1	broiler-fryer chicken (about 3 pounds), cut up
	paprika
1	small head (about 1/2 pound) green cabbage, cored and cut into 1/2-inch thick slices
	salt and pepper to taste
2	red cooking apples, cored and sliced
1	medium onion, thinly sliced
1	tablespoon grated lemon peel
2	teaspoons caraway seed
1	teaspoon sugar
1 1/2	cups (6 ounces) shredded Swiss cheese

Preheat oven to 375 degrees.

Melt butter in a large skillet with a cover. Dust chicken lightly with paprika, then place chicken in the skillet and brown on both sides over medium heat. Cover and reduce heat. Cook chicken 30 minutes.

Meanwhile, place cabbage slices on the bottom of a greased 9" x 13" baking dish. Sprinkle with salt and pepper. Cover dish with aluminum foil. Baked, covered, for 20 minutes or until cabbage is almost tender. Remove cabbage from the oven. Uncover and arrange apples and onion over cabbage. Sprinkle with lemon peel, caraway seed, and sugar. Place chicken pieces on top. Cover with foil and continue baking 25 to 30 minutes longer or until cabbage and chicken are tender. Remove from oven. Uncover and sprinkle chicken with the cheese. Return to the oven just until cheese is melted (about 5 minutes).

Serves 4 to 6.

Italian Chicken

Prepare this ahead and freeze. You'll have a real treat for drop-in guests.

1	hen (about 3 pounds)
1	package (12 ounces) egg noodles
2	tablespoons oil
4	stalks celery, chopped
2	onions, chopped
1	green pepper, chopped
3	teaspoons garlic salt
1	jar (8 ounces) chopped salad olives
1	can (8 ounces) sliced mushrooms or 1/2 pound fresh mushrooms
	juice from 1/2 lemon
	salt and pepper to taste
2	teaspoons oregano
1	can (8 ounces) tomato paste
1/2	pound sharp Cheddar cheese, grated

Clean chicken. Boil chicken in enough water to make 1 quart stock. Cool chicken in stock. Reserve stock and debone and cut up the chicken. Cook the noodles in the reserved stock.

Preheat oven to 375 degrees.

Saute celery, onions, and green pepper in oil. Add garlic salt, olives, mushrooms, lemon juice, salt, pepper, and oregano. Add chicken, tomato paste, cheese, and cooked noodles. Place mixture into a greased 2-quart casserole (or disposable aluminum container to freeze until ready to use). Bake until lightly brown and bubbly.

Serves 6.

Chicken in Lemon Sauce

Tangy and tart.

1 1/4	cup butter or margarine
4	chicken breasts , halved, boned, and skinned
2	tablespoons white wine
1/2	teaspoon grated lemon peel
1	tablespoon lemon juice
1/4	teaspoon salt
1/8	teaspoon pepper
1	cup light cream
1/3	cup grated Parmesan cheese
1	cup sliced mushrooms
	lemon wedges
	parsley

Melt butter in a large skillet over medium heat. Add chicken and saute about 10 minutes or until chicken is brown and tender. Remove chicken and place in an oblong glass baking dish. Drain butter from skillet and add wine, lemon peel, and lemon juice to the skillet. Cook 1 minute, then add salt and pepper. Pour in cream, stirring constantly, and heat but do not boil. Pour sauce over chicken. Sprinkle with cheese and mushrooms.

Set oven temperature to broil and place oven rack about 8 inches from heat. Broil until chicken is lightly brown. Garnish with lemon and parsley.

Serves 8.

Chicken Piccata

Serve with steamed broccoli and wild rice. Veal cutlets may be substituted for the chicken.

1 1/2	pounds boneless, skinless chicken breasts
	salt and pepper to taste
3	tablespoons all-purpose flour
2	tablespoons vegetable oil
4	tablespoons butter or margarine
1/3	cup chicken broth
2	teaspoons lemon juice
8	slices lemon
	chopped parsley or watercress

Flatten chicken slightly with a mallet or the side of a cleaver. Sprinkle with salt and pepper. Place flour in a paper bag, then add chicken pieces one at a time, shaking to coat.

Heat oil and butter in a large, heavy skillet over moderately high heat. Add chicken and cook about 4 minutes on each side, until lightly browned. Remove from pan and keep warm. Add chicken broth to the skillet and stir to release browned bits from bottom. Increase heat to high, add lemon juice and slices and cook for 2 minutes, until sauce is slightly syrupy. Sprinkle chicken with parsley and pour sauce over all.

Makes 4 to 6 servings.

Southern Fried Chicken

This is a family favorite, especially for my husband, Tom, and son-in-law, Gene McLamb.

1	chicken (about 2 to 2 1/2 pounds), cut into pieces
	salt and pepper
1 1/2	cups self-rising flour
1	cup cold water
	Crisco shortening

Wash chicken well. Sprinkle salt and pepper to taste over each piece.

Combine flour and water in a large bowl to make a batter. Mix thoroughly to dissolve any lumps. Add chicken.

Heat shortening in a large, heavy skillet over medium to high heat (at least 3 inches deep). Place a few chicken pieces in the skillet. Let one side brown well before turning (about 10 to 15 minutes on each side). Drain on paper towels.

Serves 4.

Cornish Hens Baked in Wine

Serve over a bed of the wild rice.

4	large (16 to 20 ounces) Cornish hens, split
	salt, pepper, paprika to taste
4	tablespoons butter or margarine
1	package (6 ounces) wild rice mixture
1	can (10 3/4 ounces) chicken broth
1	bunch green onions, sliced
6 to 8	large fresh mushrooms, sliced
1/2	cup white wine or sherry
2	bay leaves

Preheat oven to 450 degrees.

Brush hens with 2 tablespoons melted butter. Remove seasoning packet from rice mixture. Rub 1 teaspoon of seasoning on each hen. Place hens in a shallow roasting pan, breast side up. Pour chicken broth and 1/2 cup water in the pan. Bake for 15 minutes.

Meanwhile melt 2 tablespoons butter in a skillet. Add onions, mushrooms, and rice. Saute, stirring frequently. Slowly add 1 1/4 cups water, remaining seasoning from rice packet, wine and bay leaves. Bring to a boil. Pour rice mixture into the roasting pan making sure that the rice is not on top of the hens. Brush hens with the remaining butter. Cover loosely with aluminum foil. Reduce oven temperature to 350 degrees and bake an additional 45 minutes or until all liquid is absorbed.

Serves 4.

Cornish Hens with Orange Rice

Serve hens over orange rice.

1	**cup butter or margarine**
6	**cornish hens**
1	**cup apple jelly**
1/4	**cup cornstarch**
1 1/3	**cups white wine**
1/2	**cup orange juice**
	salt and pepper to taste
2	**cups white seedless grapes**

Preheat oven to 350 degrees.

Melt butter in a large skillet. Place hens in the skillet and brown. Remove hens from the skillet and place in a greased baking dish. Melt jelly and set aside. Add cornstarch to the drippings in the skillet, blending well. Add jelly, wine, orange juice, and salt. Cook on medium heat until smooth and thickened, stirring frequently. Pour sauce over the hens. Bake uncovered for 1 hour. Add grapes and bake until grapes are warmed through.

Serves 6.

Orange Rice:

2	**cups diced celery**
1/2	**cup butter or margarine, melted**
6	**tablespoons chopped onion**
2	**cups uncooked rice**
1	**teaspoon salt**
1 1/2	**cups orange juice**

Saute celery and onion in butter until tender. Add rice and salt to 2 1/2 cups boiling water. Cover and simmer about 15 minutes. Add orange juice and sauteed vegetables. Cover and cook until tender, about 5 minutes.

Serves 6.

Turkey Cutlets

A different version of turkey.

1	pound turkey cutlets
3	tablespoons all-purpose flour
	salt to taste
2	tablespoons olive oil
2/3	cup whole berry cranberry sauce
1	tablespoon lemon juice
1	teaspoon cornstarch
1	chicken bouillon cube

Pound turkey cutlets to 1/8-inch thickness with a meat mallet. Cut cutlets into 3" by 3" pieces. Combine flour and 1/2 teaspoon salt on waxed paper. Dip turkey pieces into the flour mixture to coat. Cook turkey cutlets in a nonstick skillet over medium high heat 2 to 3 minutes or until turkey is lightly browned and no longer pink. Remove to a bowl.

In the same skillet, combine cranberry sauce, lemon juice, cornstarch, bouillon cube, 1/2 teaspoon salt, and 1 cup of water. Cook, stirring constantly, until sauce boils and thickens slightly, about 1 minute. Return turkey to the skillet and heat through.

Serves 4.

Turkey Parmesan

Helen Warren from Kinston (NC) does this so well.

8	turkey breasts, cut into 3rds
2	sticks butter or margarine, melted
2	cups bread crumbs
1	teaspoon seasoned salt
1/2	teaspoon pepper
1/2	teaspoon garlic salt
3/4	cup parmesan cheese
1/4	cup parsley

Preheat oven to 350 degrees.

Place turkey breasts in the melted butter and soak for 5 minutes. Combine bread crumbs, seasoned salt, pepper, garlic salt, cheese, and parsley. Roll turkey breasts in the cheese mixture and press mixture on each piece.

Place turkey in a 9" x 13" greased baking dish. Pour remaining butter over the turkey. Bake for 45 minutes to 1 hour.

Serves 10.

Turkey Scallopini

You can use veal cutlets instead of turkey for another delicious dish.

1/4	**cup butter or margarine**
1/2	**pound thinly sliced mushrooms**
1/4	**cup all-purpose flour**
1/8	**teaspoon pepper**
1	**pound turkey cutlets**
1/4	**cup dry sherry**
	chopped parsley

Melt 2 tablespoons butter in a large, heavy skillet over medium heat. Add mushrooms and saute until tender. Remove from pan.

Combine flour and pepper and coat turkey with flour mixture, shaking off excess. Melt remaining butter in the skillet over medium heat. Brown turkey on both sides, a few pieces at a time, allowing 1 to 2 minutes per side. Remove from pan. Slowly add sherry and 1 tablespoon of water to the skillet, stirring until liquid is slightly thickened and smooth. Return turkey and mushrooms to the pan and cook until heated through.

Arrange on a serving platter and garnish with parsley.

Serves 4.

Hot Turkey Sandwiches

Great for turkey leftovers after Thanksgiving.

2	tablespoons butter or margarine, melted
2	tablespoons self-rising flour
1	cup milk
	salt and pepper to taste
	mayonnaise
4	slices toast
	sliced turkey (or chicken)
4	slices Cheddar cheese
4	slices bacon, cooked and crumbled

Melt butter in a small saucepan over low heat. Add flour, stirring until smooth. Gradually add milk, stirring until smooth and thickened. Add salt and pepper.

Spread a small amount of mayonnaise on each slice of toast. Place toast on a baking sheet. Arrange turkey on top of each slice and top with cheese. Spoon sauce over each sandwich and place under the broiler until bubbly. Sprinkle with bacon and serve immediately.

Serves 4.

Turkey Souffle

Here's something else you can do with that left over turkey ...

2	tablespoons butter or margarine
2	tablespoons self-rising flour
1	cup milk
1/2	cup turkey or chicken stock
	salt and pepper to taste
1/8	teaspoon nutmeg
1/8	teaspoon thyme
1/2	cup bread crumbs
1	cup finely chopped, cooked turkey
3	eggs, separated
3	tablespoons sherry

Preheat oven to 375 degrees.

Melt butter in a medium saucepan over low heat. Blend in flour and stir well. Gradually add milk and stock. Stir well until mixture thickens. Add salt, pepper, nutmeg, and thyme. Stir in bread crumbs alternately with turkey. Blend thoroughly. Add beatened egg yolks slowly, stirring constantly. Stir in sherry. Beat egg whites until stiff. Fold into turkey mixture. Pour mixture into a greased 2-quart souffle dish. Bake for about 30 minutes or until souffle is puffed up and brown on top.

Serves 4.

Country Style Quail

An easy way to impress your guests.

6	quail, cleaned and split
1/4	cup all-purpose flour
1	teaspoon salt
1/2	teaspoon pepper
	peanut or salad oil
	hot cooked rice
	paprika

Gravy:

3	tablespoons all-purpose flour
1/2	teaspoon salt
	pan drippings

Spread quail open and pat dry with paper towels. Combine flour, salt, and pepper. Roll quail in flour mixture, covering well. Heat about 1/4 inch oil in a skillet. Place quail in the skillet and brown on both sides, turning once. Remove from skillet and set aside.

To make the gravy, combine flour, 1 cup water, and salt, stirring until smooth. Blend flour mixture into the drippings in the skillet. Replace quail into the skillet and add enough water to cover the quail. Reduce heat to low, cover and simmer for 30 minutes or until tender. Serve quail, breast side up over hot cooked rice. Sprinkle with paprika.

Serves 6.

Seafood

Clam Fritters

Another special treat from Alice Wheatly of Beaufort (NC). These are best when served hot!

1	pint clams, drained and chopped
1/2	teaspoon salt
2	teaspoons baking powder
1/2	cup all-purpose flour
1	egg, beaten
1/4	cup evaporated milk
	cooking oil

Combine clams, salt, baking powder, flour, egg, and milk. Mix well. Heat cooking oil in a large skillet, 1/4 inch deep. Drop mixture from a spoon into the hot oil. Brown well.

Makes about 1 dozen.

Crab Cakes

Make smaller cakes and use as an hors d'oeuvre.

1	tablespoon prepared mustard
1	tablespoon fresh lemon juice
1	egg
6	tablespoons olive oil
1/2	teaspoon salt
1/2	teaspoon freshly ground pepper
1	pound lump crabmeat
1/2	cup dry, unflavored bread crumbs
	pinch of cayenne pepper
4	tablespoons butter or margarine

Combine mustard, lemon juice, and egg in a blender. While blending, gradually add 4 tablespoons olive oil. When smooth and creamy, stir in salt and pepper. Gently fold in crabmeat, bread crumbs and cayenne pepper, being careful not to break crab lumps. Shape into 8 patties, each about a 1/2 inch thick (they should just barely hold together).

Melt butter and 2 tablespoon olive oil in a skillet over medium heat. Add crabcakes and fry until golden brown, 2 to 3 minutes on each side. Drain on paper towels and serve immediately.

Serves 4.

Crab and Egg Special

Try this one for brunch - it's a winner.

1 1/2	tablespoons butter or margarine
1 1/2	tablespoons all-purpose flour
1/2	cup half-and-half
1/2	cup chicken broth
1	tablespoon sherry
1	package (6 ounces) frozen crabmeat, thawed, drained, and flaked or 1/2 pound fresh crabmeat
3	English muffins, split and toasted
6	poached eggs
1	cup (4 ounces) shredded Cheddar cheese

Melt butter in a heavy saucepan over low heat. Add flour, stirring until smooth. Cook 1 minute, stirring constantly. Gradually add half-and-half and chicken broth. Cook over medium heat, stirring constantly until thickened and bubbly. Stir in sherry and crabmeat. Cook until thoroughly heated.

Top each muffin with an egg, then spoon crabmeat over the egg. Sprinkle with cheese. Broil 1 to 2 minutes or until cheese melts. Serve immediately.

Serves 6.

Crab with Hollandaise Special

This is a quick and easy Crab Benedict!

1	**pound fresh crabmeat, drained and flaked**
1/2	**cup chopped green pepper**
1/2	**cup chopped celery**
2	**tablespoons mayonnaise**
1	**tablespoon Worchestershire sauce**
1	**tablespoon butter or margarine, melted**
1	**package (1 1/8 ounce) hollandaise sauce mix**
4	**English muffins, split and toasted**

Combine crabmeat, green pepper, celery, mayonnaise, and Worchestershire sauce. Saute mixture in butter until thoroughly heated.

Prepare hollandaise sauce according to package directions. Cut muffins in half. Spoon crabmeat mixture onto muffins and top with hollandaise sauce.

Serves 4.

Crabmeat Casserole

I have enjoyed this many times at Kate Salter's home in Beaufort (NC).

1	pound crabmeat, use more if desired
3	tablespoons lemon juice
3	teaspoons prepared spicy mustard
3	tablespoons mayonnaise
1	teaspoon finely chopped celery
1	teaspoon Worchestershire sauce
4	tablespoons butter or margarine
2	tablespoons self-rising flour
1	cup milk
	salt and pepper to taste
2	eggs, hard boiled
1/2	cup crushed potato chips

Preheat oven to 350 degrees.

Combine crabmeat, lemon juice, mustard, mayonnaise, celery, and Worchestershire sauce in a large bowl.

Prepare a white sauce by combining flour, milk, salt and pepper in a small saucepan over low heat. Whisk until sauce is thoroughly blended and slightly thickened. Pour white sauce over crabmeat mixture. Add chopped eggs and half of potato chips. Combine well and place in a 1 1/2-quart greased casserole dish. Top with remaining potato chips. Bake for 30 minutes or until bubbly and brown.

Serves 4 to 6.

Crab Souffle Casserole

Try the cabbage salad and cornbread with this.

1/2	stick butter or margarine
1/4	cup self-rising flour
1/2	teaspoon dry mustard
1	cup milk
2	tablespoons sherry
1	pound lump crabmeat, picked clean
3/4	cup shredded Cheddar cheese
2	tablespoons chopped parsley
2	tablespoons plain, dry breadcrumbs
4	large eggs, separated plus 1 egg white
1/2	teaspoon cream of tarter
	salt to taste
	dash of cayenne pepper

Melt butter in a saucepan over medium heat. Stir in flour and mustard. Cook 1 minute. Gradually stir in milk and sherry and cook, stirring constantly, until mixture boils and thickens. Remove from heat and gently stir in crabmeat, cheese, and parsley. Cool.

Preheat oven to 350 degrees.

Grease a 1 1/2-quart souffle dish. Sprinkle with bread crumbs. Beat egg whites with cream of tartar until stiff peaks form. Stir egg yolks into the crabmeat mixture. Gently fold in egg whites. Pour mixture into the souffle dish. Bake souffle 40 to 45 minutes or until a knife inserted comes out clean. Loosely cover with foil after 40 minutes if top is very brown. Serve immediately.

Serves 4.

Beer Battered Fish

This batter is good with all fish, especially catfish, grouper, and red snapper. Batter can be refrigerated up to 4 days.

	lemon juice
2	**cups self-rising flour**
1	**teaspoon salt**
1	**tablespoon paprika**
1	**can (12 ounces) beer**
	cooking oil

Dry fish thoroughly. Sprinkle lemon juice on both sides and allow to stand for 15 minutes. Combine 1 cup flour and 1 teaspoon salt and set aside. Combine 1 cup flour and paprika. Add beer and mix well. Dredge fish in dry flour mixture, then dip in beer batter.

Fry fish in 1/2 inch hot oil until golden brown on both sides. Drain on paper towels.

Serves 6 to 8.

Blackened Fish

David Greenleaf, chef at the Coral Bay Club in Atlantic Beach,
shared this Cajun secret. Prepare the seasoning mix ahead.

3/4	pound (3 sticks) unsalted butter, melted
6	fish fillets (8 to 10 ounces each), cut about 1/2 inch thick, preferably red snapper or grouper

Seasoning mix:

1	tablespoon paprika
2 1/2	teaspoons salt
1	teaspoon onion powder
1	teaspoon garlic powder
1	teaspoon cayenne pepper
3/4	teaspoon white pepper
3/4	teaspoon fresh ground black pepper
1/2	teaspoon thyme
1/2	teaspoon oregano

Heat a large cast-iron skillet over very high heat until you see white ash in the bottom of the skillet, at least 10 minutes. Meanwhile combine seasoning mix ingredients in a small bowl. Dip each fillet in the butter, so that both sides are coated. Sprinkle seasoning mix on each side, patting it in by hand.

Place fillet in the hot skillet and pour 1 teaspoon of butter on top of each filet. Cook, uncovered, over high heat until the underside of the fillets appear charred, about 2 minutes. Turn the fish over and again pour 1 teaspoon of butter on top. Cook until done, about 2 minutes more. Serve while hot with 2 tablespoons of melted butter per serving as a side dip.

Serves 6.

Grilled Mullet

This was a specialty of Dr. Theodore Salter from Beaufort (NC).
It's a real "down east" treat.

12	fresh mullets
	seasoning salt
1/2	cup vegetable oil
1	cup catsup
	dash of Worchestershire sauce
	Tabasco sauce to taste
1/2	cup white wine vinegar
	paprika

Remove heads, tails, and backbone from the mullet, but do not scale. Sprinkle each fish with seasoning salt.

Combine oil, catsup, Worchestershire sauce, Tabasco, vinegar, and paprika. Brush this mixture on each fish. Grill, scale side down, until fish flakes. Do not turn. Brush again with the sauce and serve immediately.

Serves 6.

Baked Red Snapper

This is snapper baked in a spanish (tomato) sauce.

2	pounds red snapper fillets, skinless and boneless
2	tablespoons olive oil
1 1/2	cups thinly sliced onion
2	cups (mixed) sliced sweet red and green peppers
1	tablespoon chopped garlic
1	cup sliced celery
2	cups chopped ripe tomatoes or canned tomatoes
1/4	cup capers, drained
1/4	cup chopped fresh parsley
1/2	teaspoon salt
1/2	teaspoon freshly ground pepper
1/4	teaspoon hot pepper sauce
2	tablespoon butter or margarine

Preheat oven to 425 degrees.

Cut the fish into 6 portions. Heat the olive oil in a saucepan and add onions, peppers, garlic, and celery. Cook, stirring, for 5 minutes. Add tomatoes, capers, parsley, salt, pepper, and hot sauce. Cover and cook for 12 minutes. Place the fish in a baking dish. Spoon the sauce over the fish and dot with the butter. Place the dish on the top of the stove and bring the sauce to a boil. Place the dish in the oven and bake for 12 minutes.

Serves 6.

Salmon with Sour Cream Sauce

The sauce is the secret to this salmon.

1/2	cup sour cream
1	tablespoon chopped chives
1	tablespoon milk
1/2	teaspoon finely grated lemon peel
1/2	teaspoon dried dillweed
4	fresh or frozen salmon steaks (about 1 pound), cut 1/2 inch thick
	salt to taste
2	tablespoons butter or margarine

Combine sour cream, chives, milk, lemon peel, and dillweed in a small mixing bowl. Set aside.

Rinse fish and pat dry. Sprinkle with salt. Melt butter in a skiilet over medium heat. Place salmon in the skillet and cook for 4 to 6 minutes, turning once. Serve salmon with the sour cream sauce.

Serves 4.

Salmon Souffle

Yvonne Brakehill from Raleigh (NC) shared this goody!

4	tablespoons butter or margarine
4	tablespoons finely chopped onion
4	tablespoons all-purpose flour
1	cup milk
5	eggs, separated
1	tablespoon catsup
1	can (15 ounces) salmon, drained
2	teaspoons crushed dill seed
1 1/2	teaspoons salt
2	tablespoons lemon juice
	dash cayenne pepper

Preheat oven to 400 degrees.

Grease 2 quart souffle dish with 1 tablespoon butter. Melt remaining butter in a medium saucepan. Add onion and saute for 3 minutes. Remove from heat and add flour. Stir until smooth. Add milk, stirring constantly. Return to the heat and cook until thickened.

Remove from heat and beat in egg yolks, one at a time. Stir in catsup, salmon, dill seed, salt, lemon juice, and cayenne pepper. Beat egg whites until stiff. Slowly stir into the salmon mixture. Pour into the souffle dish and place in the oven. Reduce heat to 375 degrees and bake for 30 to 40 minutes.

Serves 6.

Baked Shad

Start preparing this early ... it takes 7 hours to cook ... but it's worth it!

1	**whole shad, dressed with head and tail removed**
	salt and pepper to taste
2	**medium onions, cut into quarters**
3	**medium potatoes, cut into large cubes**
1	**stick butter or margarine, melted**
1	**can (16 ounces) whole tomatoes**
4	**slices uncooked bacon**

Preheat oven to 300 degrees.

Cut 1 1/2 inch slits in shad from neck to tail. Season with salt and pepper. Place cut side down in a baking pan. Place onions and potatoes around the fish. Combine butter and tomatoes and pour over the fish. Add enough water to cover just up to 1/2 of the fish. Place bacon slices on top. Seal baking pan with heavy aluminum foil. Bake for 7 hours. Do not open the foil during the 7 hours!

Serves 6.

Baked Fillet of Sole

The wine and grapes make this one elegant!

3	tablespoons butter or margarine
4	teaspoons all-purpose flour
1	cup dry white wine
1	teaspoon salt
1/8	teaspoon pepper
2	tablespoons chopped onion
1	teaspoon dill weed or crushed seeds
6	fillets of sole (about 1/4 pound each)
1	cup seedless green grapes

Preheat oven to 325 degrees.

Make a white sauce by melting 2 tablespoons butter in a saucepan. Add flour, mixing well. Slowly add 3/4 cup of wine, stirring constantly. Add the salt and pepper.

Melt remaining butter in a small skillet. Add onion and saute for 2 minutes. Add the dill weed and blend in the white sauce. Cook over low heat for 5 minutes or until thickened.

Roll each fillet and secure with a toothpick. Place fillets in a greased 1 1/2-quart casserole. Pour sauce over the fillets. Cook for 8 to 10 minutes or until fish flakes. Add remaining wine and sprinkle grapes on top just before serving.

Serves 4 to 6.

Trout Amandine

I like to use "speckled" trout.

3	**pounds trout fillets**
1 1/2	**cups milk**
	salt and pepper to taste
1	**cup all-purpose flour**
3/4	**cup butter or margarine**
1/2	**cup slivered almonds**
4	**tablespoons lemon juice**
2	**tablespoons Worchestershire sauce**
1 1/2	**tablespoons chopped parsley**

Cover fillets with milk. Chill for 4 hours. Drain. Season fillets with salt and pepper. Roll trout in flour.

Melt butter in a skillet, then saute trout until golden brown. Remove trout and set aside on a warm platter. Add almonds to the skillet and brown lightly, stirring constantly. Add lemon jucie, Worchestershire sauce, and parsley. Heat thoroughly and pour over the trout.

Serves 6.

Spanish Baked Trout

If you like trout, you'll love this one.

6	whole trout (about 10 ounces each), cleaned but not filleted
1/2	cup olive oil
1	teaspoon salt
1	teaspoon pepper
1 1/2	cup chopped onion
1/4	cup dry bread crumbs
1/4	cup dry white wine
2	tablespoons chopped parsley
8	slices lemon

Preheat oven to 400 degrees.

Sprinkle salt and pepper on the inside of each trout. Pour 2/3 of the oil in the bottom of a 9" x 13" baking dish. Combine with salt, pepper and onion. Spread half of onion mixture on top of oil. Arrange fish on top of onions. Brush top of fish with remaining oil. Spoon remaining onions on top of fish. Sprinkle bread crumbs over fish, then pour wine around fish. Bake uncovered for 45 minutes.

To serve, sprinkle with parsley and garnish with lemon slices.

Serves 6.

Oysters Rockefeller

This is an elegant way to present oysters.

2	packages (10 ounces each) frozen spinach, cooked
2	bunches green onion, chopped
1	stalk celery, chopped
1	bunch parsley
1	pound butter or margarne, melted
2 1/4	cups dry bread crumbs
3	tablespoons Worchestershire sauce
1	tablespoon anchovy paste
	salt to taste
	hot pepper sauce to taste
4	dozen oysters and shells
	rock salt
2	ounces Absinthe liqueur
3/4	cup Parmesan cheese

Preheat oven to 450 degrees.

Combine spinach, onion. clelery and parsley in a blender and blend well. Mix in butter and 1 1/2 cups bread crumbs. Add Worchestershire sauce, anchovy paste, salt, and hot pepper sauce. Place rock salt on the bottom of a baking pan. Place oysters (in their shells) on top of salt. Cover each oyster with sauce. Sprinkle cheese and remaining bread crumbs on each oyster. Bake until brown.

Serves 4 to 6.

Oysters Casino

So good, you may want to double the recipe.

3	slices bacon, chopped
1	stalk celery, chopped
1	teaspoon lemon juice
1	teaspoon salt
6	drops Worchestershire sauce
4	drops hot pepper sauce
1	pint oysters
	toast points

Fry bacon until partially cooked. Add onions and celery and cook until tender. Add lemon juice, salt, Worchestershire sauce, and hot pepper sauce. Arrange oysters in a well greased baking dish. Spread bacon mixture over oysters. Bake for 10 minutes or until oysters begin to curl. Serve on toast points.

Serves 4.

Escalloped Oysters

This is a must for Thanksgiving and Christmas.

2	cups saltine cracker crumbs
1/2	teaspoon salt
1/8	teaspoon pepper
1/2	cup melted butter
1	pint oysters, drained
1/4	teaspoon Worchestershire sauce
3/4	cup milk

Preheat oven to 350 degrees.

Combine cracker crumbs, salt, pepper, and butter. Sprinkle 1/3 of mixture in a buttered 2-quart casserole. Cover with a layer of oysters. Repeat with one more layer of crumbs and oysters. Add Worchestershire sauce to milk. Pour over oysters. Sprinkle remaining crumbs on top. Bake for 30 minutes.

Serves 4 to 6.

Broiled Scallops

Scallops at their best...

5	tablespoons butter or margarine
1/2	cup fresh bread crumbs
1 1/2	cups (6 ounces) shredded processed Gruyere cheese
1	cup mayonnaise
1/4	cup dry white wine
1	tablespoon chopped fresh parsley
1	pound sea scallops, quartered
1/2	pound fresh mushrooms, sliced
1/2	cup chopped onion

Preheat oven to broil.

Melt 1 tablespoon butter and toss with bread crumbs, then set aside.

Combine cheese, mayonnaise, wine, and parsley in a medium skillet over medium heat, stirring well. Cook scallops in 2 tablespoons of butter until opaque. Remove and drain well. Saute mushrooms and onion in 2 tablespoons butter for 3 minutes. Add to cheese mixture with scallops. Spoon mixture into 6 individual baking dishes. Sprinkle with bread crumbs. Broil 6 inches from source of heat for 2 to 4 minutes or until browned.

Serves 6.

Shrimp Amandine

Almonds make this one really elegant.

1	pound raw shrimp, shelled and deveined
1/4	cup olive oil
1/4	cup lemon juice
3	tablespoons butter or margarine
1	clove garlic, cut in half
1	tablespoon chopped, blanched almonds
2	dashes hot pepper sauce
2	tablespoons dry Vermouth
3	cups cooked rice

Marinate shrimp in olive oil and lemon juice for about 2 hours. Remove shrimp, reserving sauce. Saute shrimp in butter and garlic until shrimp turns pink. Remove garlic.

Place shrimp on a warm platter. Add almonds and reserved marinade to butter in the skillet. Add hot sauce and Vermouth. Let simmer for about 3 minutes. Pour over the shrimp. Serve over rice.

Serves 4.

Shrimp and Artichoke Casserole

This is also a good hors d'oeuvre served with crackers.

---

6 1/2	tablespoons butter or margarine
4 1/2	tablespoons all-purpose flour
3/4	cup milk
3/4	cup heavy cream
1	tablespoon lemon juice
	salt and pepper to taste
1/4	cup dry sherry
1	tablespoon Worchestershire sauce
1	can (14 ounces) artichoke hearts, drained
1	pound fresh shrimp (cooked, shelled and deveined)
1/4	pound fresh mushrooms, sliced
3	hard cooked eggs, chopped
1/4	cup grated Parmesan cheese
	paprika

Preheat oven to 350 degrees.

Melt 4 1/2 tablespoons butter in a saucepan. Stir in flour. Gradually add milk and cream, stirring constantly. Add lemon juice, salt and pepper. Add sherry and Worchestershire sauce.

Arrange artichoke hearts on the bottom of a 1 1/2-quart buttered baking dish. Place shrimp over artichoke hearts.

Saute mushrooms in remaining butter until tender. Spoon mushrooms over shrimp. Add eggs. Pour sauce over shrimp mixture. Sprinkle top with cheese and paprika. Bake for 25 minutes.

Serves 4.

Scallops and Mushrooms on Toast

This is a good "supper" dish.

1	**pound scallops**
	boiling salted water
3	**tablespoons butter or margarine**
1	**pound fresh mushrooms, sliced**
	salt, pepper, and paprika to taste
1 1/2	**cups chicken stock**
2	**tablespoons all-purpose flour**
1	**cup cream**
2	**egg yolks, slightly beaten**
	toast
	chopped fresh parsley

Simmer scallops in boiling water until tender.

Melt 2 tablespoons butter in a skillet. Add mushrooms, salt, pepper, and paprika and saute until tender. Blend flour and chicken stock and add to mushrooms. Add 3/4 cup cream to mushroom mixture and cook, stirring constantly, until thick and smooth. Combine mushrooms and scallops.

Combine egg yolks with remaining 1/4 cup cream. Add egg mixture and 1 tablespoon butter to the scallop mixture. Serve on toast and sprinkle with parsley.

Serves 6 to 8.

Hot Seafood Pie

This is another of Kate Salter's wonderful "down east" recipes.

2 1/2	cups crushed potato chips, divided
1/2	cup melted butter or margarine
1	pound cooked shrimp, cut into small pieces
1	pound crabmeat (or more, if desired)
1	cup finely chopped celery
1/2	cup finely chopped green pepper
1	tablespoon grated onion
2	tabespoons lemon juice
1/4	teaspoon salt
1/4	cup chopped pimento
1	cup mayonnaise
1/2	cup shredded Cheddar cheese

Preheat oven to 375 degrees.

Combine 1 1/2 cups crushed potato chips and butter. Press into a 9-inch pie plate. Bake for 5 minutes or until hardened. Cool.

Combine shrimp, crabmeat, celery, green pepper, onion, lemon juice, salt, pimento, and mayonnaise in a large bowl. Stir well. Spoon mixture into the potato chip crust. Combine remaining potato chips and cheese. Sprinkle over the top of the seafood mixture. Bake for 10 minutes or until bubbling.

Serves 6 to 8.

Shrimp Casserole

Make this is the morning and spend the rest of the day at the
bridge table.

3   pounds (medium sized) fresh shrimp
1   tablespoon lemon juice
1/2   cup chopped green pepper
1/4   cup chopped onion
2   tablespoons butter or margarine, melted
1   can (10 1/2 ounces) cream of celery soup, undiluted
1   cup light cream
1/4   cup dry sherry
1/2   teaspoon salt
1/2   teaspoon pepper
3   cups cooked rice
       paprika
2   tablespoons chopped fresh parlsey

Preheat oven to 350 degrees.

Bring 9 cups of water to a boil and add shrimp. Cook 3 to 5
minutes. Drain well, then rinse with cold water. Chill. Peel and devein
shrimp. Combine shrimp and lemon juice, set aside.

Saute green pepper and onion in butter in a small skillet until
tender. Combine soup, cream, sherry, salt and pepper. Stir in shrimp,
green pepper, onion, and rice. Spoon into lightly greased individual
au gratin dishes. Bake for 15 to 20 minutes or until bubbly. Garnish
with paprika and parsley.

Serves 6.

Shrimp and Sausage Stew

This came from, Charlie Park of Beaufort and Charlotte (NC). I could eat this stew and listen to his stories for hours!

1/4	**cup seafood boil**
3	**tablespoons coarse salt**
2	**pounds smoked sausage, cut into 2 inch pieces**
12	**ears corn, broken into 3 to 4 inch pieces**
4	**pounds fresh shrimp, unpeeled**

Combine seafood boil, salt, and 6 quarts of water in a large stockpot. Bring to a boil. Add sausage and boil for 5 minutes. Add corn and cook for 5 more minutes. Add shrimp and cook until shrimp turns pink and corn is tender, about 3 minutes. Drain immediately and serve.

This recipe can be adjusted to serve any number of people. Allow 2 teaspoons of boil per quart of water plus 1/2 pound of shrimp, 1/4 pound of sausage, and 1 1/2 ears of corn per person.

Shrimp and Grits

This is a favorite recipe of the chef David Greenleaf at the Coral Bay Club in Atlantic Beach (NC).

1	teaspoon salt
1	cup hominy grits
3/4	cup grated sharp Cheddar cheese
	hot sauce to taste
	nutmeg to taste
1	pound fresh shrimp, peeled and deveined
6	slices bacon
	peanut oil
2	cups sliced fresh mushrooms
1	cup finely sliced green onions
1	large garlic clove, minced
4	teaspoons lemon juice
2	tablespoons fresh, chopped parsley
	salt and pepper to taste

Add 4 1/2 cups water and salt to a large saucepan. Bring to a boil. Stir in grits. reduce heat. Simmer for 30 minutes, stirring frequently, until mixture is thickened. Blend in cheese, stirring until melted. Add small amount of hot sauce, nutmeg and pepper to taste.

Dice bacon and saute lightly in a skillet (bacon should not be crisp). Add enough peanut oil to the bacon fat to make a layer of about 1/8 inch deep. When very hot, add shrimp in an even layer. Turn shrimp as they start to turn pink. Add mushrooms and saute for 4 minutes. Add onions and garlic. Season with lemon juice, additional hot sauce, and salt and pepper. Serve shrimp immediately over the grits.

Serves 4.

Shrimp in Remoulade Sauce

This is good as a "first" course.

1	package (3 1/4 ounces) crab and shrimp boil mix
1	tablespoon salt
1	onion, quartered
1	clove garlic
1	lemon, sliced
3	pounds fresh shrimp
6	tablespoons tarragon vinegar
3	tablespoons creole mustard
4	green onion with tops, minced
1	stalk celery, minced
2/3	cup olive oil
	lettuce
2	hard cooked eggs, sliced
1	avocado, peeled and sliced in wedges

Bring 3 quarts of water to a boil. Add crab and shrimp boil mix, salt, onion, garlic, lemon slices, and shrimp. Cover and simmer 5 minutes. Drain and chill. Peel and devein shrimp.

Combine vinegar, mustard, onion, celery, and olive oil. Mix well. Pour sauce over shrimp, coating shrimp thoroughly. Cover and refrigerate for several hours. Toss shrimp and serve on lettuce and garnish with egg and avocado wedges.

Serves 8.

Shrimp Creole

A green salad and french bread complete this meal.

2	slices bacon
2	tablespoons butter or margarine
1	green pepper, coarsely chopped
1	onion, coarsely chopped
3	stalks celery, coarsely chopped
3	cloves garlic, minced
5	fresh tomatoes, peeled and chopped or 2 cups canned tomatoes
	salt and pepper to taste
	hot pepper sauce to taste
1/2	cup chicken stock
1 1/2	pounds shrimp (cooked, peeled, and deveined)
2	tablespoons finely chopped fresh parsley
	juice of 1/2 lemon
3	cups cooked white rice

Fry bacon and set aside. Add green pepper, onion, celery, garlic, and tomatoes to the bacon grease and saute for 10 minutes or until just tender. Add salt, pepper, hot sauce, and chicken stock and cook for another 5 minutes. Add shrimp and cook 3 to 5 minutes or until shrimp are heated through. Add parsley and lemon juice. Serve over rice.

Serves 6.

Shrimp Bake

Prepare ahead and enjoy!

2	pounds shrimp, cooked
1	clove garlic
2	tablespoons all-purpose flour
2	tablespoons butter or margarine
1	cup cream
1/2	teaspoon salt
1/4	teaspoon pepper
	paprika
1/2	cup tomato sauce
2	tablespoons Worchestershire sauce
	buttered bread crumbs

Preheat oven to 400 degrees.

Rub saucepan well with garlic. Melt butter and add flour, mixing well. Gradually add the cream, stirring constantly. Cook until thick and smooth. Add shrimp, salt, pepper, paprika, tomato sauce, and Worchestershire sauce. Mix well. Fill individual baking dishes with shrimp mixture. Sprinkle tops with bread crumbs. Bake for 10 minutes.

Serves 8 to 10.

Shrimp and Crabmeat Casserole

This is an easy way to feed a crowd.

2	cups chopped onion
2	cups chopped celery
1	green pepper, chopped
1/4	cup butter or margarine, melted
2	cups wild rice, cooked
2	pounds, shrimp (cooked, peeled, and deveined)
1	jar (2 ounces) sliced pimento, drained
1	pound crabmeat
3	cans (10 3/4 ounces) cream of mushroom soup, undiluted
1	can (8 ounces) sliced mushrooms, drained
3/4	cup slivered, toasted almonds
1	cup bread crumbs

Preheat oven to 325 degrees.

Saute onion, celery, and green pepper in butter until tender. Add wild rice, shrimp, pimento, crabmeat, soup, and almonds. Pour mixture into 2 lightly greased 2-quart casseroles. Sprinkle each with bread crumbs. Bake for 1 hour until brown and bubbly.

Serves 16.

Shrimp with Linguine

This is a quick and light main dish that has it all. Just serve with a salad and your favorite bread and you've got a meal!

1/4	cup butter or margarine
3	cloves garlic, minced
1 1/2	pounds medium sized shrimp, uncooked but peeled and deveined
1	package (10 ounces) snow peas, thawed
1/2	cup sliced green onions
1	cup sliced fresh mushrooms
1/4	cup lemon juice
3	tablespoons chopped fresh parsley
1 1/2	teaspoons seasoned salt
1/2	teaspoon pepper
3	cups hot cooked linguine

Melt butter in a large skillet. Add garlic and saute. Add shrimp, snow peas, onions, and mushrooms, stirring for 5 minutes. Add lemon juice, parsley, salt and pepper. Toss well and serve over linguine.

Serves 4 to 6.

Shrimp with Garlic

*Serve this over your favorite pasta, such as angel hair or
vermicelli, or rice. Another quick shrimp dish!*

1	**tablespoon olive oil**
1	**pound shelled shrimp, deveined**
2	**cloves garlic, minced**
2	**teaspoons capers, chopped**
1	**tablespoon lemon juice**
2	**teaspoons butter or margarine, melted**

Add oil to a large skillet over medium heat. Add shrimp and
garlic and cook for 6 to 8 minutes or until shrimp just start to turn pink.
Stir constantly. Add lemon juice and capers and mix well. Stir in butter
and serve.

Serves 4 to 6.

Shrimp Neuberg

This tastes great served over rice or in individual patty shells with rice as a side dish.

2	tablespoons butter or margarine
2	tablespoons all-purpose flour
1	cup half and half
3	tablespoons catsup
1	tablespoon Worchestershire sauce
1	pound shrimp (cooked, peeled, and deveined)
	salt and pepper to taste
4	tablespoons sherry

Melt butter in a large skillet. Stir in flour. Add cream, stirring constantly, until thickened and smooth. Add catsup, Worchestershire sauce, and shrimp. Heat through. Add salt and pepper. Just before serving, add sherry.

Serves 4.

Breakfast, Brunch, and Lunch

Breakfast Casserole

This is a favorite of both family and friends.

6	**slices bread, crusts removed, buttered on one side**
1	**pound pork sausage, cooked and drained**
1	**small onion, diced**
1 1/2	**cups shredded Cheddar cheese**
6	**eggs, beaten**
2	**cups half and half**
1	**teaspoon salt**

Line bottom of a greased 9" X 13" baking dish with bread, buttered side up. Spread sausage and onion evenly over the bread. Sprinkle cheese over the sausage. Combine eggs, cream and salt. Mix well and pour over the cheese. Cover and chill overnight.

Preheat oven to 350 degrees.

Bake for 45 minutes or until golden brown.

Serves 8.

Spanish Breakfast Casserole

Breakfast with a kick.

12	eggs, beaten
2	cans (17 ounces) cream style corn
2	cans (4 ounces) chopped green chilies, drained
2	cups shredded extra sharp Cheddar cheese
2	cups shredded Monterey Jack cheese
1	tablespoon instant grits
1 1/2	teaspoons Worchestershire sauce
	hot pepper sauce to taste

Preheat oven to 325 degrees.

Combine eggs, corn, green chilies, cheeses, grits, Worchestershire sauce and hot pepper sauce in a large bowl. Mix well. Pour into a greased 1 1/2-quart baking dish. Bake 1 hour or until firm to the touch and lightly browned.

Serves 8.

Cheesy Grits Souffle

This is good with ham, seafood, you name it - it's just good.

1	**cup uncooked regular grits**
2	**cups milk**
2	**cups water**
	salt and pepper to taste
1/2	**teaspoon hot pepper sauce**
2	**cups grated sharp Cheddar cheese**
6	**large eggs, separated**

Preheat oven to 425 degrees.

Butter a 2-quart souffle dish and place in the freezer until ready to use. Place grits, milk and water in a large saucepan and cook according to directions on the package. Add salt to taste. Place cooked grits into a large mixing bowl. Add pepper and hot sauce to taste. Stir in 1 1/2 cups cheese. Let cool slightly. Slightly beat eggs yolks and add to grits mixture, stirring until well blended.

Beat egg whites until stiff. Add half of the egg whites to the grits mixture, mixing well. Gently fold in remaining egg whites. Spoon mixture into the souffle dish and smooth over the top. Sprinkle remaining cheese on top. Bake for 30 minutes.

Serves 6.

Cajun Grits Souffle

Why not dress up those ol' grits?

1/3	cup self-rising white corn meal
1	teaspoon salt
1/3	cup quick grits
2	cups grated sharp Cheddar cheese
1/8	teaspoon cayenne pepper
4	eggs, separated
1/2	teaspoon cream of tartar

Preheat oven to 350 degrees.

Combine 2 2/3 cups water, corn meal, and salt in a large saucepan. Bring to a boil. Slowly stir in grits. Cover and cook for 5 to 6 minutes or until thickened. Add cheese and cayenne pepper and stir until cheese is melted. Cool 10 minutes. Stir in beaten egg yolks. Beat egg whites until stiff. Add cream of tartar. Fold egg whites into grits mixture. Pour into an ungreased 2-quart casserole. Bake for 55 minutes.

Serves 4 to 6.

Cherry Coffee Cake

You can substitute any fruit of your choice for the cherry pie filling.

1	package yellow cake mix, divided
1	cup all-purpose flour
1	package active dry yeast
2	large eggs, beaten
1	can (21 ounces) cherry pie filling
1/3	cup butter or margarine

Glaze:

1	cup powdered sugar
4 to 6	teaspoons milk

Preheat oven to 375 degrees.

Combine 1 1/2 cups cake mix, flour, and yeast in a bowl. Add 2/3 cup **warm** water, stirring until smooth. Stir in eggs. Spoon batter into a greased 9" X 13" pan . Spread pie filling evenly over the batter. Cut butter into remaining cake mix with a fork until mixture is crumbly. Sprinkle over pie filling. Bake for 25 to 30 minutes. While cooling, prepare glaze by combining sugar and milk, stirring until smooth. Drizzle over cake.

Serves 6 to 8.

Apple Crunch Coffee Cake

Do ahead and enjoy.

2	cups Bisquick
2/3	cup milk
3	tablespoons sugar
1	egg
2	medium cooking apples, peeled and thinly sliced
3	tablespoons chopped pecans

Topping:

3/4	cup self-rising flour
3/4	cup packed brown sugar
1	teaspoon cinnamon
1/2	teaspoon ground nutmeg
1/4	cup butter or margarine

Glaze:

1/2	cup confectioners' sugar
2	teaspoons milk

Preheat oven to 400 degrees.

Combine Bisquick, milk, sugar, and egg and mix well. Spread half of mixture into a greased 9" x 9" pan. Arrange apple slices on batter. Sprinkle with half of topping. Pour remaining batter over mixture and sprinkle with remaining topping. Cover with pecans. Bake for 25 minutes or until done. Let cool for a few minutes. Combine confectioners' sugar and milk and drizzle glaze over the top.

Serves 8.

Cheese Omelet

There's nothing better!

1/4	pound sliced bacon
6	eggs
1/2	teaspoon salt
1/4	teaspoon pepper
1	tablespoon cream
1/8	pound Swiss cheese, grated
2	tablespoons chopped chives
2	tablespoons butter or margarine

Cook bacon in a skillet until crisp. Drain, crumble and set aside. Beat eggs with 1 tablespoon cold water, salt and pepper. Stir in cream and half of the crumbled bacon, half of the cheese, and 1 tablespoon of chives.

Melt butter in an omelet pan or a 10" skillet. Pour in the egg mixture all at once. Cook over medium heat. As omelet sets, run spatula around edge to loosen. Tilt pan to let uncooked portion run underneath. Continue until the omelet is almost dry on top and golden brown on the bottom. Sprinkle with the remaining bacon, cheese and chives. To turn out, loosen edge with a spatula . Fold in half and tilt onto plate.

Serves 2.

Basic Omelet

This is a good recipe for a basic omelet. My favorite topping is a Spanish Omelet. Make your choice on the next page!

1/2	**teaspoon salt**
4	**eggs, separated**
1/8	**teaspoon pepper**
1	**tablespoon butter or margarine**

Combine salt, 1/4 cup water and egg whites and beat until stiff. Add pepper to egg yolks and beat until thick. Fold egg whites into egg yolks.

Melt butter into an omelet pan or 10" skillet. Pour in omelet mixture. Cook over medium heat. As omelet sets, run spatula around edge to loosen. Tilt pan to let uncooked portion run underneath. Continue until the omelet is almost dry on top and golden brown on the bottom. To turn out, loosen edge with a spatula . Fold in half and tilt onto plate. Cover with topping.

Serves 2.

Spanish Omelet Topping I

*This was created by the late Mrs. Fitzhugh Wallace of Kinston
(NC). Her daughter, Mrs. Erwin Parrot, has shared this often.*

1	can (14 1/2 ounces) tomatoes, chopped
2	small green peppers, chopped
1	small can (2 ounces) pimentos, drained
2	small onions, chopped
1	small bottle (5 ounces) stuffed olives, chopped
1	cup cooked green peas
1/2	pound sharp Cheddar cheese, grated
	salt and pepper to taste
	cayenne pepper to taste

Combine tomatoes, green peppers, pimentos and onions in a saucepan. Simmer for 20 minutes. Add olives and peas. Pour over basic omelet and sprinkle with cheese. Leftovers freeze well.

Makes approximately 3 cups.

Spanish Omelet Topping II

1	tablespoon butter or margarine
2	tablespoons minced onion
2	tablespoons minced green pepper
3	cans (8 ounces) tomato sauce
1	tablespoon Worchestershire sauce
1/8	teaspoon cayenne pepper

Melt butter in a saucepan and saute onion and green pepper for 3 minutes. Add tomato sauce, Worchestershire sauce and cayenne pepper. Simmer for 20 minutes or until sauce is thickened. Pour over basic omelet.

Makes enough for 2 omelets.

Blueberry Pancakes

Serve with crispy bacon or your favorite sausage.

1	**cup milk**
1	**egg**
1/4	**cup sour cream**
1	**cup all-purpose flour**
1	**tablespoon baking powder**
1	**tablespoon sugar**
1/4	**teaspoon salt**
2	**tablespoons butter or margarine, melted**
1/2	**cup fresh blueberries**

Combine milk, egg, and sour cream in a bowl and mix well. Combine flour, baking powder, sugar and salt. Add flour mixture to milk mixture. Beat just until large lumps disappear. Stir in butter. Fold in blueberries. Pour about 1/4 cup of batter for each pancake into a hot, lightly greased skillet. Turn pancakes when tops are covered with bubbles.

Makes 12 pancakes.

Potato Pancakes

You can substitute left over mashed potatoes and not have to
place the mixture in a blender - but be sure to dice the onions.

2	**cups peeled and diced potatoes**
2	**eggs**
2	**slices medium onion, peeled**
1	**teaspoon salt**
	pepper to taste
1/4	**cup all-purpose flour**
1/4	**teaspoon baking powder**
	cooking oil
	applesauce or sour cream

Place 1 cup of potatoes, eggs, onion, salt and pepper in a blender. Cover and blend at high speed for 5 seconds. Add flour, baking powder and remaining potatoes. Cover and blend at high speed until potatoes are just grated.

Heat oil in a skillet. Spoon by tablespoonfuls into skillet and cook until golden brown, turning once. Serve with applesauce or sour cream.

Serves 6 to 8.

French Toast

When serving this, please include me on your guest list!

1/2	stick butter or margarine, softened
12	slices French bread, 3/4 inch thick
6	eggs
2	cups milk
1/2	cup sugar
2	tablespoons maple syrup
3	teaspoons vanilla
1/2	teaspoon salt
1/2	teaspoon cinnamon (optional)
	confectioners' sugar
	maple syrup, heated

Spread butter over the bottom and sides of a large baking dish. Arrange bread slices on dish. Combine eggs, milk, sugar, syrup, vanilla, salt, and cinnamon (if desired). Beat well. Pour mixture over bread. Turn bread to coat on both sides. Cover and refrigerate overnight.

Preheat oven to 400 degrees.

Bake bread mixture for 10 minutes. Turn bread over and continue baking for 5 additional minutes. Remove bread from dish onto a serving platter. Sprinkle with powdered sugar. Serve immediately and pass the maple syrup!

Serves 6.

Welsh Rarebit

A cheesy delight.

1	**teaspoon dry mustard**
1	**teaspoon paprika**
1/2	**teaspoon salt**
3/4	**pound extra sharp Cheddar cheese**
1/2	**cup beer, at room temperature**
1	**teaspoon Worchestershire sauce**
	dash of red pepper
1	**egg**
4	**slices tomato**
4	**slices bread, toasted**
4	**slices bacon, cooked and halved**

Combine mustard, paprika and salt in a small bowl and smooth out lumps. Add 1/2 cup beer, Worchestershire sauce, and egg. Stir until well mixed. Melt cheese in a chafing dish or the top of a double broiler. Add beer mixture to the cheese, stirring well until smooth. Add more beer, if needed. Cook until slightly thickened, stirring constantly.

To serve, place a tomato slice on each slice of bread. Top each tomato with 2 bacon halves. Spoon cheese sauce over bacon and serve immediately.

Serves 4.

_____

_____

_____

_____

_____

_____

_____

_____

_____

_____

Breads

Breads •

Easy to Make Corn Bread

We've enjoyed this at Kate Salter's house in Beaufort (NC) many times. It's so good, you might need to make a double recipe.

1	package Flake Corn Muffin mix
1	can (8 1/2 ounces) cream style corn
1	container (8 ounces) sour cream
1	egg
1	stick butter or margarine, melted

Preheat oven to 350 degrees.

Combine muffin mix, corn, sour cream, egg and butter in a mixing bowl. Pour batter into a greased 9" x 9" baking pan. Bake for 20 minutes or until golden brown. Slightly cool before removing from the pan.

Serves 4 to 6.

Fried Corn Bread

This is a favorite of the whole family. If you like very thin corn bread, add a little more water.

	shortening for frying
1 1/4	cups self-rising white corn meal
1	cup boiling water
2	tablespoons bacon grease, melted
1	egg
2	tablespoons minced onion

Melt shortening in a heavy skillet, 1/4-inch deep, and heat over medium heat.

Combine corn meal and hot water in a small bowl, stirring well. Add bacon grease, egg, and onion. Place batter in the hot shortening, 1 teaspoonful at a time. Corn bread will brown quickly. Turn over once and brown on the other side. Drain on paper towels. Serve while hot.

Serves 4.

You can make hushpuppies by slightly changing this recipe. Combine 2 cups of corn meal and 1 1/2 to 2 cups boiling water. Add the egg, onion and bacon grease. Batter should be slightly thick. Drop by rounded tablespoonful into deep hot fat and fry until golden brown (about 3 to 4 minutes). Serve hot. Makes 2 dozen.

Spoon Bread

This southern recipe came from Marilyn Roper of Charlottesville (VA) and Atlantic Beach (NC). Great with pork and fish.

2	**cups milk**
1/2	**teaspoon salt**
3/4	**cup plain white corn meal**
4	**tablespoons butter, cut up**
4	**eggs**
1	**teaspoon baking powder**
	softened butter

Preheat oven to 325 degrees.

Combine milk and salt in a saucepan and bring to a boil. Reduce heat and stir in corn meal. Continue stirring about 4 minutes until mixture thickens. Stir in 4 tablespoons butter and remove from heat. Beat eggs with baking powder and stir into the corn meal mixture.

Pour mixture into a greased 2-quart casserole. Bake for 60 minutes. Serve with softened butter.

Serves 6 to 8.

Angel Biscuits

These are more like rolls than biscuits.

5	cups all-purpose flour
1/4	cup sugar
3	teaspoons baking powder
1	teaspoon salt
1	teaspoon baking soda
1	cup shortening
1	package dry yeast
2	cups buttermilk

Preheat oven to 375 degrees.

Combine flour, sugar, baking powder, salt, and soda in a mixing bowl. Cut in shortening with a fork.

Dissolve yeast in 2 tablespoons warm water. Add yeast and buttermilk to flour mixture, mixing well. Cover and store mixture in the refrigerator 8 hours or overnight.

Remove from the refrigerator. Roll out, approximately 1/2 " thick, and cut with a biscuit cutter. Brush with melted butter and let rise 1 1/2 to 2 hours. Bake for 10 to 15 minutes or until golden brown.

Makes 3 to 4 dozen.

Baking Powder Biscuits

This is a good basic recipe for biscuits.

2	**cups all-purpose flour**
3	**teaspoons baking powder**
1/2	**teaspoon salt**
1/3	**cup shortening**
3/4	**cup milk**

Preheat oven to 400 degrees.

Combine flour, baking powder and salt. Cut in shortening with a fork until mixture resembles coarse corn meal. Pour in milk, a little at a time. Mix well until dough consistency. Add additional milk, if necessary.

Roll out dough on a lightly floured surface, about 1/2-inch thick. Cut with a biscuit cutter. Place biscuits on an ungreased cookie sheet. Bake for 15 minutes.

Make about 1 1/2 dozen.

Cheese Biscuits

Cheese turns a plain biscuit into a treat.

1	**cup self-rising flour**
1	**cup grated sharp Cheddar cheese**
1/4	**teaspoon baking powder**
1/3	**cup shortening**
1/4	**milk (may need a little more)**

Preheat oven to 400 degrees.

Combine flour, cheese and baking powder in a mixing bowl. Cut in shortening. Add enough milk to make a dough.

Roll out dough on a lightly floured surface, about 1/2-inch thick. Cut with a biscuit cutter. Place biscuits on an ungreased cookie sheet. Bake for 15 minutes.

Makes about 1 dozen.

€asy Muffins

This easy (but so good and rich) to make recipe was shared by
Peggy Haigler of Raleigh (NC).

1   **stick butter, softened**
4   **ounces sour cream**
1   **cup self-rising flour**

Preheat oven to 375 degrees.

Combine butter, sour cream and flour in a bowl and mix well.
Spoon mixture into ungreased, miniature muffin tins, filling about 3/4
full. Bake for 10 minutes or until brown.

Makes 24.

Apple Muffins

These go well with pork chops.

1	cup all-purpose flour
1/4	cup instant mashed potato granules
3	tablespoons sugar
1	tablespoon baking powder
1/2	teaspoon salt
1	tart cooking apple, peeled and finely diced
1	egg, slightly beaten
1	cup milk
1/4	cup butter or margarine, melted
1/4	teaspoon cinnamon

Preheat oven to 425 degrees.

Combine flour, potato granules, 2 tablespoons sugar, baking powder, salt and apple in a bowl.

Lightly beat together egg, milk, and butter. Add to flour mixture and stir until just blended. Spoon into 12 to 15 well greased muffin tins.

Combine remaining 1 tablespoon sugar with cinnamon. Sprinkle over muffins. Bake for 15 to 20 minutes or until golden brown.

Makes 12 to 15 muffins.

Miniature Banana Muffins

So moist and tasty!

---

1 1/2	cups all-purpose flour
1/2	cup sugar
2	teaspoons baking powder
1/2	teaspoon baking soda
1/2	teaspoon salt
1/2	cup golden raisins
1	tablespoon grated orange rind
2	medium ripe bananas, well mashed
1	cup sour cream
1	egg
1/2	stick butter or margarine, melted and cooled

Preheat oven to 400 degrees.

Sift flour, sugar, baking powder, soda, and salt in a large bowl. Add raisins and orange rind.

Combine bananas, sour cream, egg and butter in a small bowl. Add all at once to the flour mixture. Stir lightly. Batter will be lumpy. Spoon equally greased miniature muffin tins, filling 2/3 full. Bake for 20 minutes or until golden brown.

Makes 24 muffins.

Blueberry Muffins

Keep these in the freezer to pull out for company!

2 1/2	cups all-purpose flour
2 1/2	teaspoons baking powder
1	cup sugar
1/4	teaspoon salt
1	cup buttermilk
2	eggs, beaten
1/4	pound butter or margarine, melted
1 1/2	cups fresh or frozen blueberries, rinsed and drained

Preheat oven to 400 degrees.

Sift flour, baking powder, sugar, and salt together into a large bowl. Add buttermilk, eggs, and butter. Mix well. Fold in blueberries. Fill greased muffin tins half full and bake for 20 minutes. Serve warm.

Makes 24 small muffins.

Bran Muffins

Good and healthy, too.

1	**cup All-Bran cereal**
1	**cup raisins**
1 1/2	**cups sugar**
1/2	**cup Crisco**
2	**eggs**
2 1/2	**cups all-purpose flour**
2 1/2	**teaspoons baking soda**
2	**cups buttermilk**
2	**cups 40% Bran Flakes cereal**
1	**cup chopped pecans**

Preheat oven to 400 degrees.

Combine 1 cup boiling water, All-Bran, and raisins in a bowl and let stand.

Cream sugar and Crisco in a large mixing bowl. Add eggs one at a time. Sift flour and baking soda together. Add to sugar mixture alternately with the buttermilk. Mix well. Add Bran Flakes and pecans. Stir in the bran and raisin mixture.

Fill greased muffin tins 2/3 full. Bake for 20 minutes.

Makes 3 dozen.

Apricot-Nut Bread

Once again, apricots really do make a difference.

1	can (16 ounces) apricot halves
1/2	cup sugar
1/3	cup Crisco
2	eggs
1 3/4	cups all-purpose flour
1	teaspoon baking powder
1/2	teaspoon baking soda
1/2	teaspoon salt
1/2	cup chopped pecans

Preheat oven to 350 degrees.

Drain apricots, reserving liquid. Place apricots in a blender or food processor to puree. Combine enough reserved liquid with the apricots to make 1 cup and set aside.

Cream sugar and Crisco until fluffy. Add eggs, one at a time, beating well after each addition.

Combine flour, baking powder, baking soda, and salt. Add flour mixture and apricots alternately to creamed sugar mixture. Stir just until all ingredients are moistened. Stir in pecans. Spoon batter into a greased 9" x 5" loaf pan. Bake for 50 minutes or until cake tester inserted into center comes out clean. Remove from pan and cool on a wire rack.

Makes 1 loaf.

Date-Nut Bread

This is good with cream cheese as a sandwich or as an hors d'oeuvre.

1	package dates, pitted and chopped
1/2	cup orange juice
4	tablespoons butter or margarine
1	cup sugar
2	eggs
4	cups all-purpose flour
2	teaspoons salt
1	teaspoon cinnamon
1/2	teaspoon nutmeg
1/2	teaspoon cloves
2	cups chopped pecans

Preheat oven to 325 degrees.

Combine 1 cup boiling water, dates and orange juice in a bowl. Let stand for 20 minutes.

Cream butter and sugar until fluffy. Add eggs, one at a time, beating well after each addition. Combine flour, salt, cinnamon, nutmeg and cloves. Stir flour mixture into butter mixture alternately with liquid from dates. Mix in dates and pecans. Bake for about 1 hour or until cake tester inserted into center comes out clean.

Makes 2 loaves.

Monkey Bread

Don't tell your guests how easy this is to make.

1   **cup sugar**
1   **teaspoon cinnamon**
3   **cans biscuits**
1   **stick butter or margarine**
1/2   **cup brown sugar**

Preheat oven to 350 degrees.

Place 1/2 cup sugar and cinnamon in a plastic bag. Cut each biscuit into 4 pieces. Place biscuit pieces in plastic bag and shake well with cinnamon mixture. Drop biscuit pieces into a greased and floured bundt pan.

Combine 1/2 cup sugar, butter, and brown sugar in a saucepan over medium heat. Bring to a boil. Pour over the biscuit pieces. Bake for 30 to 40 minutes.

Sesame-Cheese Bread

Try this for breakfast.

3	**tablespoons sesame seeds**
1	**egg, beaten**
1 1/2	**cups milk**
3 3/4	**cups Bisquick**
1	**cup shredded Cheddar cheese**
1	**tablespoon chopped fresh parsley**
1/4	**teaspoon pepper**

Preheat oven to 350 degrees.

Sprinkle sesame seeds onto the bottom and sides of a greased 2-quart casserole.

Combine egg, milk, Bisquick, cheese, parsley and pepper. Beat well. Pour mixture into the casserole. Bake for 40 to 45 minutes or until cake tester inserted into center comes out clean. Immediately remove bread from the casserole and cool on a wire rack.

Makes 1 loaf.

Apple Fritters

These are good with pork.

1/2	cup milk
1	egg
2	tablespoons butter or margarine, melted
	grated rind from 1/2 orange
	juice from 1/2 orange
1/2	cup chopped apples
1/2	teaspoon vanilla
1 1/2	cups cake flour
1/2	cup sugar
1/4	teaspoon salt
1	tablespoon baking powder
	hot vegetable or peanut oil

Combine milk and egg in a bowl. Add butter, orange rind, orange juice, apples and vanilla.

Sift together flour, sugar, salt, and baking powder. Stir milk mixture into the flour mixture until blended. Do not over mix.

Drop batter by spoonfuls into 1/2-inch of oil, heated to 375⁰, in a heavy skillet. Fry until golden brown. Drain on a paper towel and serve hot.

Make approximately 12 fritters.

Banana Fritters

These are almost like dessert.

1 3/4	cups Bisquick
1/2	cup milk
2	eggs
4	bananas, peeled and sliced
	hot vegetable or peanut oil
	confectioners' sugar

Combine Bisquick, milk, and eggs and blend well. Add bananas and stir gently to coat. Drop each coated slice into deep oil heated to 375 degrees. Fry until golden bown, turning once. Drain on paper towels. Sprinkle with confectioners' sugar. Serve hot.

Makes about 3 dozen.

Corn Fritters

These are good with fish and pork.

1	cup all-purpose flour
1	teaspoon baking powder
3/4	teaspoon salt
1/2	teaspoon paprika
2	eggs, separated
2	tablespoons milk
2	cups cooked, drained corn
	hot vegetable or peanut oil

Combine flour, baking powder, salt and paprika. Add egg yolks and milk, mixing well. Stir in corn. Beat egg whites until stiff and fold into batter.

Heat 2 inches of oil to 375 degrees in a heavy skillet. Drop by spoonfuls into the hot oil and fry until golden brown. Drain on apaper towels. Serve hot.

Makes 2 dozen.

Dressings and Sauces

Curry-Poppy Seed Fruit Dressing

This dressing keeps indefinitely in the refrigerator.

1/2	cup sugar
1/2	cup honey
1	teaspoon grated onion
6	tablespoons tarragon vinegar
3	tablespoons lemon juice
1	cup salad oil
1	teaspoon dry mustard
1	teaspoon paprika
1/4	teaspoon salt
2	teaspoons poppy seeds
1	teaspoon curry powder

Combine sugar, honey, onion, vinegar, lemon juice, oil, mustard, paprika, salt, poppy seeds, and curry powder in a jar with a top. Shake well. Use over fresh or frozen fruit.

Makes about 2 cups.

Roquefort Dressing

Serve over your favorite green salad.

3/4	cup mayonnaise
1/3	cup sour cream
1	package (1 1/2 ounces) Roquefort cheese, crumbled
1	teaspoon Worchestershire sauce
	dash of garlic powder
	salt and pepper to taste

Combine mayonnaise, sour cream, cheese, Worchestershire sauce, garlic powder, salt and pepper and stir well. Chill thoroughly in a covered container.

Makes about 1 1/2 cups.

Sour Cream Dressing

This is good with fish.

1/2	cup mayonnaise
1/2	cup sour cream
1	teaspoon mustard
1	teaspoon finely chopped olives
1/4	teaspoon sugar

Combine mayonnaise, sour cream, mustard, olives, and sugar and mix well. Chill thoroughly in a covered container.

Makes 1 cup.

Tarragon Vinegar Dressing

Serve over a salad of boston lettuce, avocado, spring onions and croutons.

6	**tablespoons olive oil**
2	**tablespoons tarragon vinegar**
1	**teaspoon salt**
1	**teaspoon Accent**
	dash of garlic salt

Combine oil, vinegar, salt, Accent, and garlic salt in a covered jar. Shake well before serving.

Makes 1/2 cup.

Thousand Island Dressing

Serve over your favorite green salad.

1/2	cup mayonnaise
1	tablespoon chili sauce
1	tablespoon finely chopped celery
1	tablespoon finely chopped pimento
1	tablespoon finely chopped green pepper
1	tablespoon coarsely chopped hard cooked egg

Combine mayonnaise. chili sauce, celery, pimento, green pepper, and egg and mix well. Chill in a covered container.

Makes 3/4 cup.

Vinaigrette Dressing

This tastes great over chilled asparagus spears as a salad.

1	**cup French dressing**
1	**teaspoon finely chopped olives**
1	**teaspoon capers**
1	**teaspoon chives**
1	**teaspoon parsley**
1	**hard cooked egg, chopped**

Combine French dressing, olives, capers, chives, parsley and egg. Chill in a covered container.

Makes 1 cup.

Barbecue Sauce I

Charlotte Herring from Kinston (NC) shared this. It is good with chicken. You can refrigerate the sauce up to 1 month.

1 1/2	cups vinegar
4	tablespoons sugar
3	tablespoons mustard
1	teaspoon black pepper
3	teaspoons salt
3/4	teaspoon cayenne pepper
2	thick lemon slices
1/2	cup butter
1/2	cup catsup
4	tablespoons Worchestershire sauce

Preheat oven to 350 degrees.

Combine vinegar, sugar, mustard, black pepper, salt, cayenne pepper, lemon, butter, catsup, and Worchestershire sauce in a saucepan. Add 3/4 cup water. Simmer for 20 minutes. Do not boil.

Makes about 3 cups.

Barbecue Sauce II

This is daughter Jess McLamb's favorite. Brush over chicken or pork for a tangy taste.

1 1/2	cups vinegar
1	teaspoon black pepper
1	teaspoon salt
2	teaspoons crushed red pepper
1/2	cup butter or margarine
1 1/2	cups catsup
3	tablespoons Worchestershire sauce

Combine vinegar, pepper, salt, red pepper, butter, catsup and Worchestershire sauce in a saucepan. Simmer for 20 minutes. Do not boil.

Makes about 4 cups.

Beef Marinade

This will help to make less expensive cuts of beef as tender as fillet.

1	cup salad oil
1/3	cup wine or tarragon vinegar
1	cup red wine
1	teaspoon garlic powder
1/2	teaspoon pepper
1	package Good Seasons Italian dressing mix
1	bay leaf
1	onion, sliced

Combine oil, vinegar, wine, garlic powder, pepper, dressing mix, and onion. Pour over meat. Let meat remain in marinade for at least 2 hours. Turn meat several times.

Makes 2 1/2 cups.

Bernaise Sauce

Serve with steaks and pork chops.

2	**tablespoons white wine**
1	**tablespoon tarragon vinegar**
2	**teaspoons chopped fresh tarragon or 1 teaspoon dried tarragon**
2	**teaspoons chopped onion**
1/4	**teaspoon black pepper**

Combine wine, vinegar, tarragon, onion, and pepper in a skillet. Bring to a boil. Cook rapidly until the mixture is reduced to 1 teaspoon. Combine mixture with 1 1/4 cups Hollandaise sauce in an electic blender. Cover and blend on high speed for 4 seconds.

Makes 1 1/4 cups.

Bordelaise Sauce

Serve this hot over your favorite roast or broiled beef.

2	tablespoons butter or margarine
2	tablespoons all-purpose flour
1	tablespoon minced onion
1	tablespoon minced parsley
1/4	teaspoon thyme
1/8	teaspoon coarsely ground black pepper
1	bay leaf
1	can (10 1/2 ounces) beef broth, undiluted
1/4	cup dry red wine

Melt butter in a heavy 1-quart saucepan over low heat. Add flour and cook stirring often, until slightly brown. Stir in onion, parsley, thyme, pepper, and bay leaf.

Slowly add beef broth and red wine. Stir mixture to blend well. Increase heat to medium high. Cook, stirring constantly, until the mixture boils and thickens. Boil 1 minute. Discard bay leaf.

Makes about 1 1/3 cups.

Hollandaise Sauce

Serve over asparagus, brocolli, eggs benedict, and more.

3	egg yolks
2	tablespoons lemon juice
1/4	teaspoon salt
1/2	cup butter or margarine, melted

In an electric blender, blend egg yolks, lemon juice, and salt. Using low speed, slowly add hot butter. To keep warm, place in a heatproof container and place container in a saucepan of hot water. If sauce gets too thick, add 1 or 2 teaspoons water, then beat until smooth.

Makes 1 cup.

Foolproof Mock Hollandaise Sauce

This is a slightly different version, but you'll never fail to make this perfect every time!

3   **egg yolks, beaten**
       juice from 1 lemon
1   **cup sour cream**
       salt, pepper, and sugar to taste

Combine eggs yolks and lemon juice in the top of a double boiler. Add sour cream, salt, pepper, and sugar. Let cook over medium heat for about 5 minutes or until thickened, stirring constantly. Serve immediately or reheat over water when ready to serve.

Makes 2 cups.

Horseradish Sauce

Serve with prime rib of beef or fish.

1   cup heavy cream, whipped until stiff
2   teaspoon grated onion
4   tablespoons horseradish
2   tablespoons minced parsley
        sea salt to taste

Place cream in a mixing bowl. Fold in onion, horseradish, parsley, and salt. Cover and refrigerate 30 minutes.

Makes 1 1/2 cups.

Mustard Sauce

Serve with roast beef or pork, or as a sauce with hors d'oeuvres.

2	**egg yolks, beaten**
1	**tablespoon sugar**
3	**tablespoons mustard**
2	**tablespoons vinegar**
1	**tablespoon butter or margarine**
1	**tablespoon horseradish**
1/2	**teaspoon salt**
1/2	**cup heavy cream, whipped**

Combine egg yolks, sugar, mustard, vinegar, butter, horseradish, salt, and 1 tablespoon water in a double broiler. Simmer until thick and smooth, stirring constantly. Fold in whipped cream. Refrigerate in a covered container.

Makes 1 cup.

Sweet and Sour Sauce

Add to your favorite cuts of chicken or pork for a Chinese touch.

2	green peppers, cut into strips
2	cups pineapple chunks
3/4	package brown sugar
3	tablespoons molasses
2	cups vinegar
1	teaspoon salt
	pepper to taste
2	tablespoons cornstarch

Combine green pepper, pineapple, brown sugar, molasses, vinegar, salt and pepper with 1 1/2 cups water in a saucepan. Bring to a boil. Simmer 5 minutes.

Combine cornstarch with 1/4 cup water. Combine with green pepper mixture. Cook until thickened, stirring constantly.

Makes about 3 cups.

Tartar Sauce

Serve with your favorite seafood.

1	tablespoon chopped parsley
2	cloves garlic
5	small sweet pickles, chopped
3	pitted olives, chopped
1	teaspoon tarragon
1	teaspoon black pepper
1 1/4	cups mayonnaise

Combine parsley, garlic, pickles, olives, tarragon, pepper, and mayonnaise in a blender. Blend at high speed for 6 seconds.

Makes 1 1/2 cups.

Mayonnaise

Probably high in calories, but you can't beat the taste!

1/2	teaspoon salt
1	teaspoon mustard
1/8	teaspoon pepper
1/8	teaspoon paprika
1/4	teaspoon sugar
2	eggs
2	cups salad oil
3	tablespoons lemon juice

Combine salt, mustard, pepper, paprika, sugar, and egg in a mixing bowl and beat well with an electric mixer. Gradually add 1/2 cup oil, drop by drop. Add lemon juice and remaining oil very slowly, beating well after each addition. Beat until stiff.

Makes 2 1/2 cups.

Desserts, Candies, and More

Apple Pie

Rome or Granny Smith apples are best.

3/4	**cup brown granulated sugar**
1	**tablespoon all-purpose flour**
1/2	**teaspoon cinnamon**
1/4	**teaspoon nutmeg**
1/8	**teaspoon salt**
1	**tablespoon grated lemon peel**
6	**cups peeled, cored and thickly sliced apples**
1	**tablespoon lemon juice**
2	**tablespoons butter or margarine**
2	**uncooked pastry shells (9-inch)**

Preheat oven to 425 degrees.

Combine sugar, flour, cinnamon, nutmeg, salt and lemon peel in a large bowl. Add apples and toss to coat evenly. Pour apple mixture into a pastry shell. Sprinkle with lemon juice and dot with butter. Top with remaining pastry shell. Trim and flute edges. Cut a vent in the top with a knife to allow steam to excape. Bake for 40 minutes or until golden brown. Cool.

Serves 6 to 8.

Banana Cream Pie

If you have any leftovers, they'll keep well in the refrigerator for just a few days.

3	tablespoons cornstarch
1	can (14 ounces) sweetened condensed milk
3	eggs yolks, beaten
2	tablespoons butter or margarine
1	teaspoon vanilla
3	medium bananas
	lemon juice
1	baked pastry shell (9-inch)
1	cup heavy cream, whipped

Dissolve cornstarch in 1 2/3 cups water in a saucepan. Stir in milk and egg yolks. Cook until bubbly, stirring constantly. Remove from heat and add butter and vanilla.

Slice 2 bananas. Dip in lemon juice and arrange on bottom of the prepared crust. Pour filling over bananas. Chill for 4 hours or until set.

Spread whipped cream over the top. Slice remaining banana and dip slices in lemon juice. Place on top of whipped cream as garnish.

Serves 8.

Chocolate-Banana Cream Pie

Chocolate makes everything better.

1/2	cup sugar
1/3	cup cornstarch
1/2	teaspoon salt
2 1/2	cups milk
1	cup semi-sweet chocolate pieces
1	teaspoon vanilla
3	eggs yolks, slightly beaten
1	baked pastry shell (9-inch) or graham cracker crust
2 to 3	medium bananas
1/2	cup heavy cream, whipped
	chopped nuts, if desired

Combine sugar, cornstarch and salt in a saucepan. Add milk gradually, stirring constantly. Add chocolate and vanilla. Continue cooking over medium heat, stirring constantly. Bring to a boil and boil for 1 minute. Remove from heat .

Stir a small amount of the egg yolk into the hot mixture. Mix well, then add remaining egg yolks. Cook over low heat for 5 minutes or until thickened.

Pour half of mixture into prepared pie shell. Slice the bananas and layer over the chocolate filling. Pour remaining chocolate mixture over the bananas, spreading evenly.

Place wax paper directly over pie and refrigerate until well chilled and filling is set, approximately 3 hours or longer.

To serve, decorate edge with whipped cream and top with nuts, if desired.

Serves 8.

Brandy Alexander Pie

A dessert fit for royalty.

1	envelope unflavored gelatin
2/3	cup sugar
3	eggs, separated
1/8	teaspoon salt
1/4	cup cognac
1/4	cup Creme de Cacao
1	cup whipping cream, whipped
1	graham cracker crust (9-inch)
3	squares (1 ounce each) semisweet chocolate

Combine gelatin and 1/2 cup cold water in a small saucepan. Let stand 5 minutes. Stir in 1/3 cup sugar, egg yolks, and salt. Cook over low heat, stirring constantly until gelatin dissolves and mixture thickens. Do not boil. Remove from heat and add cognac and Creme de Cacao. Chill about 25 to 45 minutes or until mixture is slightly thickened.

Beat egg whites until stiff. Gradually add 1/3 cup sugar, stirring constantly. Fold egg whites into gelatin mixture. Fold in whipped cream. Pour mixture into crust. Garnish with chocolate curls. Chill overnight.

Serves 8.

> *To make chocolate curls, melt chocolate squares. Pour the melted chocolate onto wax paper and spread to a 3-inch wide strip. Let stand until cool but not firm. Pull a vegetable peeler over the chocolate and transfer the curls to a plate. Store chocolate curls in the freezer.*

Chocolate Coffee Pie

This is really rich and yummy.

Crust:
2	egg whites
1/8	teaspoon cream of tartar
1/2	cup sugar
2	packages (3 ounces) finely chopped blanched almonds

Filling:
1	cup sugar
1	envelope unflavored gelatin
	pinch of salt
2	eggs, separated
1	cup milk
1	package (12 ounces) semisweet chocolate chips
1/4	cup coffee liqueur
1	cup heavy whipping cream
1	teaspoon vanilla

For crust: Preheat oven to 375 degrees. Beat egg whites until foamy. Add cream of tartar. Gradually add sugar and continue beating until stiff. Fold in almonds. Spread mixture over the bottom and sides of an oiled 10-inch pie pan. Bake for 15 to 20 minutes or until lightly browned. Cool.

For filling: Place 1/4 cup sugar, gelatin, and salt in top of a double boiler. Beat egg yolks and milk together, then add to gelatin. Cook until slightly thickened, stirring constantly. Add chocolate chips and continue cooking until chocolate has melted. Cool. Stir in coffee liqueur.

Beat egg whites until foamy. Slowly add 1/2 cup sugar and continue beating until whites are stiff. Fold into chocolate mixture. Whip cream. Add 1/4 cup sugar and vanilla when cream is partially beaten. Spoon chocolate mixture and cream alternately into the pie shell. Swirl with spoon to create a marbling effect. Cool until firm.

Serves 8.

Creamy Chocolate Pie

This is a quick and easy favorite of my daughter-in-law, Sue Roper, from Burgaw.

6	milk chocolate candy bars (1.45-ounce) with almonds
1	carton (8 ounces) frozen whipped topping, thawed
1	baked pastry shell (9-inch)
3	squares semisweet chocolate

Place candy bars and 2 tablespoons hot water in the top of a double broiler. Bring the water to a boil. Reduce heat to low and cook until candy bars are melted. Cool about 20 minutes. Gradually fold in whipped topping. Spoon into pastry shell. Chill for 8 hours.

Garnish with chocolate curls.

Serves 6 to 8.

> To make chocolate curls, melt chocolate squares. Pour the melted chocolate onto wax paper and spread to a 3-inch wide strip. Let stand until cool but not firm. Pull a vegetable peeler over the chocolate and transfer the curls to a plate. Store chocolate curls in the freezer.

Coconut Cream Pie

This tastes best if you make and serve it the same day.

1/2	cup sugar plus 6 tablespoons
5	tablespoons all-purpose flour
1/8	teaspoon salt
1	cup shredded coconut
1/4	cup cold milk
1 1/2	cup milk, scalded (heated just to the boiling point)
3	egg yolks, separated
1	teaspoon vanilla
1	baked pastry shell (9-inch)

Preheat oven to 300 degrees.

Blend 1/2 cup sugar, flour, and salt with cold milk. Gradually add to scalded milk and cook over low heat until thickened. Beat egg yolks and add to mixture. Cook 2 minutes longer. Remove from heat and add vanilla and coconut. Cool. Pour into the pastry shell.

Beat egg whites until stiff. Gradually add 6 tablespoons sugar, stirring constantly. Pour over coconut mixture. Bake about 20 minutes or until lightly browned.

Serves 8.

Daiquiri Pie

This is a great summer treat ... light and fun!

1	package (3.4 ounces) lemon pudding mix
1	package (3 ounces) lime gelatin
1/3	cup sugar
2	eggs, slightly beaten
1/2	cup light rum
2	cups non-dairy frozen whipped topping, thawed
1	baked graham cracker crumb crust (9-inch)
	lime slices

Combine pudding mix, gelatin, and sugar in a saucepan. Stir in 1/2 cup water and eggs. Blend well. Add 2 cups of water. Stir over medium heat until mixture comes to a full boil. Remove from heat and stir in rum. Chill for 1 1/2 hours.

Blend topping with pudding mixture. Spoon into crust. Chill for 2 hours or until firm. Garnish with additional whipped topping and lime slices.

Serves 6 to 8.

Eggnog Pie

This is a great holiday treat.

1	**tablespoon unflavored gelatin**
1/3	**cup sugar**
2	**tablespoons cornstarch**
1/8	**teaspoon salt**
2	**cups prepared eggnog**
1 1/2	**squares unsweetened chocolate, melted**
1	**teaspoon vanilla**
6	**tablespoons rum**
1	**graham cracker crumb crust (9-inch)**
2	**cups heavy cream, whipped**
1/4	**cup confectioners sugar**

Sprinkle gelatin in 1/4 cup cold water.

Combine sugar, cornstarch, and salt in the top of a double broiler. Gradualy stir in the eggnog, stirring constantly, until thickened. Remove from heat and stir in gelatin. Divide filling in half.

Add melted chocolate and vanilla to one half. Set aside. Allow remaining half to cool and add 2 tablespoons of rum and whipped cream. Pour rum flavored mixture into the pie shell. Then pour chocolate mixture on top. Chill overnight. Top with 1 cup whipped cream mixed with confectioners sugar and 4 tablespoons of rum. Garnish with chocolate curls.

Serves 6 to 8.

Grasshopper Ice Cream Pie

Your guests will think you've worked long and hard, but only you will know it was easy to make!

1	pint vanilla ice cream, softened
2	tablespoons lemon juice
2	tablespoons Creme de Menthe
2	tablespoons Creme de Cacao
1	container frozen non-dairy whipped topping, just thawed
1	chocolate crumb crust (9-inch)
3	squares semisweet chocolate

Combine ice cream, lemon juice, Creme de Menthe, and Creme de Cacao in a bowl. Fold in whipped topping, blending well. Spoon into crust. Freeze 4 hours or until firm. Garnish with chocolate curls. Store leftovers in the freezer.

Serves 8.

To make chocolate curls, melt chocolate squares. Pour the melted chocolate onto wax paper and spread to a 3-inch wide strip. Let stand until cool but not firm. Pull a vegetable peeler over the chocolate and transfer the curls to a plate. Store chocolate curls in the freezer.

Lemon Chess Pie

This is a good standby that is loved by even the most discriminating guest.

2	cups sugar
1	tablespoon all-purpose flour
1	tablespoon cornmeal
4	eggs, unbeaten
1/4	cup butter, melted
1/4	cup milk
4	tablespoons grated lemon rind
1/4	cup lemon juice
1	unbaked pastry shell (9-inch)

Preheat oven to 375 degrees.

Combine sugar, flour and cornmeal in a large bowl. Add eggs, butter, milk, lemon rind and lemon juice. Beat until well blended.

Continue stirring as you pour into the pastry shell. Bake for 35 to 45 minutes or until knife blade inserted in the center comes our clean.

Serves 6 to 8.

To make individual lemon tarts, pour filling into 6 to 8 unbaked tart shells. Bake at 350° for 30 to 45 minutes or until set.

Lemon Puff Pie

A little different from a lemon meringue pie and just as tangy.

6	eggs, separated
1	cup sugar plus 1 tablespoon
	grated rind of 1 lemon
5	tablespoons lemon juice
1	baked pastry shell (9-inch)
1/4	teaspoon salt

Preheat oven to 350 degrees.

Beat eggs yolks until thickened. Gradually beat in 1/2 cup sugar. Add lemon rind, lemon juice, and 2 tablespoons water. Cook over low heat, stirring constantly until thickened. Cover and cool.

Beat 4 egg whites until soft peaks form. Gradually beat in 1/2 cup sugar. Beat until stiff. Fold into egg yolk mixture. Turn into the pastry shell.

Beat 2 remaining eggs whites with salt until frothy or soft peaks form. Gradually add remaining sugar. Beat until stiff. Drop heaping teaspoonfuls of this meringue in 10 or 12 mounds around the edge of the pie. Bake until meringue is lightly browned.

Serves 6 to 8.

Easy to Make Lime Pie

This is a "must do" for guests ... and it looks elegant, too.

1	can (6 ounces) frozen limeade concentrate, undiluted
1	can (14 ounces) sweetened condensed milk
1/4	cup sour cream
2 to 3	drops green food coloring
3	cups (8-ounce carton) frozen non-dairy topping, thawed
1	prepared chocolate flavored pie crust
	chocolate chips for garnish

Combine limeade and milk. Add sour cream and food coloring, stirring until well blended. Fold in thawed whipped topping. Spoon the filling into the pie crust, mounding the filling high above the rim of the crust. Swirl the top. Chill for 6 hours or until set.

Garnish with chocolate chips.

Serves 6 to 8.

Margarita Pie

Includes everything but the salt!

1	envelope unflavored gelatin
1	cup sugar
1	teaspoon salt
4	eggs, separated
1	cup freshly squeezed lime juice
1/3	cup tequila
2	tablespoons orange liqueur
2	teaspoons grated lime peel
1	baked pastry shell (10-inch)
1/4	cup whipping cream, whipped and sweetened to taste
8	lime peel twists

Combine gelatin, 1/2 cup sugar, and salt in a heavy saucepan.

Beat egg yolks and lime juice together until foamy. Stir into gelatin mixture. Cook about 3 minutes over low heat until gelatin is dissolved. Stir in tequila, orange liqueur, and lime peel. Cool and refrigerate until mixture is thick but not set.

Beat egg whites until foamy. Slowly add remaining 1/2 cup sugar and continue beating until stiff peaks form. Fold egg whites into gelatin mixture. Turn into pie crust and chill thoroughly.

Spoon whipped cream around edge of pie and garnish with lime peel twists.

Serves 6 to 8.

Hot Mincemeat Pie

When Christmas is coming, this is a necessity.

2 unbaked pastry shells (9-inch)
1 egg white, slightly beaten
1 jar (1pound, 12 ounces) prepared mincemeat
1/2 cup applesauce

Sauce:
1/3 cup granulated sugar
1/3 cup light brown sugar, firmly packed
1 lemon wedge
1 orange wedge
1/4 cup dark rum

Preheat oven to 375 degrees.

Brush inside of pastry shell with egg white. Combine mincemeat and applesauce in a bowl, then turn into pastry shell. Place second pie shell over the top of the mincemeat mixture. Pinch the edges together and make 3 knife slits in the top.

Bake for 30 minutes.

Meanwhile prepare the sauce by combining sugars with 1 cup water. Cook over low heat until sugar is dissolved. Bring to a boil. Add lemon and orange wedges. Reduce heat and simmer for 30 minutes. Discard lemon and orange wedges. Add rum just before serving.

Serve pie warm with some sauce over each serving.

Serves 8.

Pecan Pie

This is a favorite of my son-in-law, Gene McLamb of Raleigh (NC), so I usually keep one in the freezer for unexpected visits.

1/4	**cup butter or margarine**
1/2	**cup sugar**
1	**cup dark corn syrup**
1/4	**teaspoon salt**
3	**eggs**
1	**cup pecan halves**
1	**unbaked pastry shell (9-inch)**

Preheat oven to 350 degrees.

Cream butter. Add sugar gradually and cream until fluffy. Add syrup and salt and beat well. Add eggs one at a time, beating thoroughly after each egg. Stir in pecans. Pour into the pie shell. Bake for 45 minutes or until a knife inserted halfway between outside and center of filling comes out clean.

Serves 6 to 8.

Pecan Fudge Pie

A chocolate lover's version of pecan pie.

1	**package (4 ounces) sweet cooking chocolate**
1/4	**cup margarine or butter**
1	**can sweetened condensed milk**
2	**eggs, well beaten**
1	**teaspoon vanilla**
1 1/4	**cups pecan pieces**
1	**unbaked pastry shell (9-inch)**

Preheat oven to 350 degrees.

Combine and melt chocolate and butter in a medium saucepan over low heat. Stir in milk, 1/2 cup hot water, and eggs, mixing well. Remove from heat and add vanilla and pecans. Pour into pastry shell. Bake for 40 to 45 minutes or until a knife inserted halfway between outside and center of filling comes out clean. Cool. Chill for 3 hours.

Serves 6 to 8.

Frozen Peanut Butter Pie

This is a very rich, but very easy to fix, dessert.

1   package (4 ounces) cream cheese, softened
1   cup confectioners sugar
1/3   cup peanut butter
1/2   cup milk
1   container frozen non-dairy topping, thawed
1   graham cracker crust (9-inch)
           chopped peanuts

Combine cream cheese, sugar, and peanut butter until well blended. Add milk and topping, blending well. Pour into crust. Sprinkle peanuts on top. Freeze.

Serves 8.

Pumpkin Chiffon Pie

You don't have to wait for the holidays to make this favorite. My daughter, Jess McLamb of Raleigh (NC), loves this year round!

3	egg yolks
1	cup sugar
1 1/4	cups cooked pumpkin
1/2	cup milk
1/2	teaspoon salt
1/2	teaspoon ginger
1	teaspoon cinnamon
1/2	teaspoon nutmeg
1	teaspoon rum flavoring
1	tablespoon plain gelatin, dissolved in 1/4 cup cold water
3	egg whites
1	graham cracker crust (9-inch)
1	container non-dairy whipped topping, thawed

Beat egg yolks then add 1/2 cup sugar. Beat until mixed well. Stir in pumpkin, milk, salt, ginger, cinnamon, and nutmeg. Cook in top of a double boiler until thick. Add dissolved gelatin. Cool slightly.

Beat egg whites until stiff. Gradually add 1/2 cup sugar. Fold egg whites into cooled pumpkin mixture. Pour into crust. Chill for 3 hours before serving. Serve with whipped topping.

Serves 8.

Pumpkin Pecan Pie

*My daughter likes pumpkin pie. My son-in-law likes pecan pie. So
we make this one to please both of them.*

3	tablespoons butter or margarine
2/3	cup firmly packed brown sugar, divided
1/3	cup chopped pecans
1	unbaked pastry shell (9-inch)
3	eggs
1 1/2	cups canned pumpkin
1/2	cup granulated sugar
1	teaspoon salt
1 1/2	teaspoons pumpkin pie spice
1	cup evaporated milk
1/2	cup heavy cream, whipped

Preheat oven to 450 degrees.

Cream butter with 1/3 cup of the brown sugar. Add pecans
and press onto bottom of pastry shell. Bake shell for 10 minutes and
cool. Reduce oven heat to 350 degrees.

Beat eggs slightly. Stir in pumpkin, remaining brown sugar,
granulated sugar, salt and pumpkin pie spice. Dilute milk with 1/2 cup
water and heat until scalded (just before boiling). Add milk to pumpkin
mixture and beat well. Pour mixture into the pie shell. Bake about 50
minutes or until center is soft but set. Serve warm (not hot) with
whipped cream.

Serves 8.

Sweet Potato Pie

This was another recipe from my grandmother, Liza Wooten, of Kinston (NC).

2	cans (16-17 ounces) vacuum packed sweet potatoes
1/2	cup packed brown sugar
1/2	cup milk
2	eggs
2	tablespoons butter or margarine, melted
2	tablespoons lemon juice
3/4	teaspoon salt
1/4	teaspoon cinnamon
1	unbaked pie crust (9-inch)

Preheat oven to 400 degrees.

Mix sweet potatoes, sugar, milk, eggs, butter, lemon juice, salt, and cinnamon in a large bowl. Spoon into pie crust. Bake for 45 minutes or until set. Serve hot or cold.

Serves 8.

Strawberry Cheese Pie

When strawberry season arrives, this is a must!

1	package (8 ounces) cream cheese
1	can sweetened condensed milk
1/3	cup lemon juice
1	teaspoon vanilla
1	graham cracker crust (9-inch)
1	quart fresh strawberries, cleaned and hulled
1	package (16 ounces) prepared strawberry glaze, chilled

Beat cheese in a large bowl until fluffy. Gradually beat in milk. Stir in lemon juice and vanilla. Pour into crust. Chill for 3 hours or until set.

Top with strawberries and glaze. Refrigerate leftovers.

Serves 8.

Apple Dapple Cake

This yummy recipe came from Donna Perry, an interior decorator from Youngesville (NC), and a friend of my daughters.

3	eggs
2	cups sugar
1 1/2	cups vegetable oil
1	cup pecans pieces
3	cups all-purpose flour
1	teaspoon salt
1	teaspoon baking soda
1	teaspoon baking powder
1	teaspoon cinnamon
1	teaspoon allspice
3	cups peeled, cored and diced apples

Topping:

1	cup dark brown sugar
1/2	cup milk
1	stick butter or margarine

Preheat oven to 350 degrees.

Combine eggs, sugar, oil, pecans, flour, salt, soda, baking powder, cinnamon, and allspice in a large bowl, mixing well. Blend in apples. Pour into a greased 10-inch tube pan. Bake for 45 minutes or until a toothpick comes out clean when inserted into cake.

Prepare topping by combining sugar, milk and butter in a saucepan. Bring to a boil and cook for 2 minutes. Pour over hot cake.

Serves 8 to 10.

Banana Spice Cake

This is a spicy, moist treat.

---

1 1/2	**cups sugar**
1/2	**cup butter or margarine**
2	**eggs, beaten**
2 1/4	**cups cake flour**
1/2	**teaspoon baking powder**
3/4	**teaspoon baking soda**
1/2	**teaspoon salt**
1/2	**teaspoon nutmeg**
1/2	**teaspoon cinnamon**
1/2	**teaspoon cloves**
1/4	**cup buttermilk**
1	**cup mashed bananas**
1	**teaspoon vanilla**

Preheat oven to 350 degrees.

Cream sugar and butter. Add eggs. Sift together flour, baking powder, baking soda, salt, nutmeg, cinnamon, and cloves. Add to sugar mixture alternately with the buttermilk. Blend thoroughly. Add bananas and vanilla. Pour into 2 greased and floured 8-inch cake pans. Bake for 30 minutes or until lightly browned and cake springs back when lightly touched.

Frost with an icing of your choice.

Serves 8 to 10.

Cheese Cake

Straight from New York ...

2	envelopes unflavored gelatin
1	cup sugar
1/2	teaspoon salt
2	eggs, separated
1	cup milk
1	teaspoon grated lemon rind
3	cups cottage cheese
1	tablespoon lemon juice
1	cup whipping cream
1	teaspoon vanilla
1/2	teaspoon nutmeg

Crumb Topping:

1/2	cup graham cracker crumbs
2	tablespoons butter or margarine, melted
1	tablespoon sugar
1/2	teaspoon cinnamon
1/2	teaspoon nutmeg

Combine gelatin, 3/4 cup sugar, and salt in the top of a double boiler. Beat together egg yolks and milk. Add to the gelatin mixture. Cook over boiling water, stirring constantly, for about 6 minutes or until gelatin is thoroughly dissolved. Remove from heat and add lemon rind. Chill until mixture mounds slightly when dropped by a spoon.

While mixture is chilling, beat cottage cheese on high speed with an electric blender for 3 to 5 minutes. Stir in lemon juice, vanilla, and nutmeg. Beat egg whites until stiff. Beat in remaining 1/4 cup sugar and continue beating until sugar is dissolved. Beat whipping cream until stiff. When gelatin mixture is chilled, stir in cottage cheese mixture until well mixed. Fold in egg whites and whipped cream. Pour into an 8" springform pan.

Combine crumb topping ingredients and sprinkle over the top of the cake. Chill until set.

Serves 8 to 10.

Cream Cheese Cupcakes

These are great for gifts or for hors d'oeuvres.

3/4	cup graham cracker crumbs
2	tablespoons butter, melted
3	packages (8 ounces each) cream cheese, softened
1	teaspoon plus 3/4 cup sugar
1 1/2	teaspoons vanilla
3	eggs
1	can (20 ounces) prepared cherry pie filling
	paper cupcake liners

Preheat oven to 325 degrees.

Combine graham cracker crumbs, butter and 1 teaspoon sugar in a mixing bowl. Place cupcake liners in muffin tins. Place 1/2 teaspoon of crumb mixture in each liner. Pat down.

Combine cream cheese, vanilla, 3/4 cup sugar, and eggs in a mixing bowl. Blend well until mixture is very smooth. Pour on top of crumbs, filling liners about half full. Bake for 20 to 25 minutes or until lightly browned. Cool. Top with pie filling.

Makes 18 cupcakes.

Chocolate Amaretto Cheesecake

Amaretto lovers will love this.

6	chocolate wafers, finely crushed
1 1/2	cups light cream cheese
1	cup sugar
1	cup low-fat cottage cheese
1/3	cup plus 2 tablespoons unsweetened cocoa
1/4	cup all-purpose flour
1/4	cup amaretto
1	teaspoon vanilla
1/4	teaspoon salt
1	egg
2	tablespoons chocolate mini-morsels

Preheat oven to 300 degrees.

Sprinkle chocolate wafer crumbs in the bottom of a 7" springform pan. Set aside.

Place the knife blade in your food processor. Add cream cheese, sugar, cottage cheese, cocoa, flour, amaretto, vanilla, and salt. Blend until smooth. Add egg and process until blended. Fold in chocolate morsels.

Pour mixture over crumbs in the pan. Bake for 65 to 70 minutes or until cheesecake is set. Cool in the pan, then cover and chill for at least 8 hours.

Serves 12.

Chocolate Refrigerator Cake

You won't believe how easy this is.

2	eggs, separated
1	package (8 to 10 ounces) semisweet chocolate bits
1	teaspoon vanilla
	pinch of salt
1	large angle food cake
1	cup whipping cream, whipped

Beat egg whites until stiff and set aside.

Melt chocolate. Add egg yolks to the chocolate. Add vanilla and salt. Fold in egg whites and whipped cream.

Break cake into bite size pieces. Place a layer of cake pieces in the bottom of a springform pan. Cover with half of the chocolate mixture. Repeat layers of cake and chocolate mixture. Refrigerate for several hours.

Unmold to serve. Garnish with additional whipped cream.

Serves 8.

Easy German Chocolate Cake

Your guests won't know you didn't spend hours on this! My daughter, Jess McLamb, first put this together for an office party.

1   box German chocolate cake mix

Topping:
1   stick butter or margarine
1   cup evaporated milk
1   cup sugar
1   cup chopped pecans
1   bag (6 ounces) coconut

    Prepare cake mix according to directions on the box. Pour the batter into a greased 9" x 13" pan and bake according to directions.

    Prepare topping while cake is cooking by melting butter in a medium saucepan. Add milk and sugar and cook over medium heat until sugar is melted. Stir in pecans and coconut.

    Prick the top of the cake with a toothpick. Pour topping over the hot cake, spreading evenly.

    Serves 12.

Chocolate Rum Cake

This keeps well in the refrigerator for several days.

1 box chocolate cake mix
1 package (3.4 ounces) chocolate instant pudding mix
4 eggs
1 cup rum
1/2 cup vegetable oil

Filling:
1 1/2 cups milk
1/4 cup rum
1 package (3.4 ounces) chocolate instant pudding mix
1 envelope whipped topping mix

Preheat oven to 350 degrees.

Combine cake mix, pudding mix, eggs, rum and oil in a bowl and blend well. Pour into 2 greased 9" cake pans. Bake for 30 minutes or until a toothpick comes out clean when placed in the center of each cake. Cool for ten minutes in the pans, then place on racks to continue cooling.

While cakes are cooling, combine the milk, rum, pudding mix, and topping mix to make the filling. Blend until light and fluffy.

Split layers horizontally. Spread topping between each layer and over the top of the cake. Cover and refrigerate until ready to serve. Serve cold and refrigerate leftovers.

Serves 8 to 10.

Chocolate Cake

Another chocolate lover's favorite.

1	stick butter or margarine
1	cup sugar
4	eggs
1	cup self-rising flour
1	can (16 ounces) Hersey's chocolate syrup
1	teaspoon vanilla

Icing:

1	stick butter or margarine
1	cup sugar
1/3	cup evaporated milk
1/2	cup chocolate chips
1/2	cup chopped pecans

Preheat oven to 325 degrees.

Cream butter and sugar thoroughly in a mixing bowl. Add eggs, one at a time, beating constantly. Add flour alternately with syrup. Mix well, then add vanilla. Pour into a greased and floured bundt pan. Bake for 45 minutes. Cool slightly, then remove from pan to cool further.

While cake is cooling, prepare icing. Combine butter, sugar, and evaporated milk in a saucepan. Bring to a boil and boil for 2 minutes. Remove from heat and add chocolate chips and pecans. Spread over cake.

Serves 8 to 10.

Sour Cream Chocolate Cake

So moist, so easy, why not make two and freeze one?

1	box chocolate cake mix
4	eggs
1/2	cup vegetable oil
1	package (3.4 ounces) chocolate instant pudding mix
1	container (8 ounces) sour cream
1/2	cup chopped pecans
1	teaspoon vanilla
1	bag (6 ounces) chocolate chips

Icing:

1	stick butter or margarine
1	cup brown sugar
1/4	cup evaporated milk
	confectioners sugar, sifted

Preheat oven to 350 degrees.

Combine cake mix, eggs, oil, pudding mix, 1/4 cup water, and sour cream in a mixing bowl. Blend well.

Add pecans, vanilla, and chocolate chips. Pour into a greased and floured 10-inch tube pan. Bake for 1 hour. Cool slightly, then remove from pan to cool further.

While cake is cooling, prepare icing. Combine butter and sugar in a saucepan. Heat until bubbling. Remove from stove and add milk. Add enough confectioners sugar until mixture is of spreading consistency. Spread over cake.

Serves 8 to 10.

Easy Coconut Cake

This easy recipe came from Lib Honeycutt from Greenville (NC). She says you can substitute fresh coconut if you have it.

1	box yellow cake mix
2	cups sugar
2	cups sour cream
2	packages (9 ounces each) frozen coconut, thawed
1 1/2	cups frozen non-dairy whipped topping, thawed

Bake cake as directed on the package using 2 layer pans. Let cake cool, then split layers horizontally.

While cake is cooking, combine sugar, sour cream, and coconut in a bowl, mixing well. Chill. Spread coconut topping on each layer. Spread whipped topping on the tops and sides of the cake.

Store in the refrigerator at least 24 hours before serving.

Serves 8.

Crumb Cake

Annalea Hunneke from Kinston (NC) shared this from her Kappa Alpha Theta cookbook. This is a great dessert or brunch cake.

2	cups brown sugar
2	cups all-purpose flour
1/2	cup butter or margarine
1	egg
1	cup buttermilk
1	teaspoon baking soda
1/8	teaspoon salt
	cinnamon
	granulated sugar

Preheat oven to 350 degrees.

Combine sugar, flour, and margarine together using a pastry blender or your hands. Measure 1 cup of crumbs and set aside.

Combine remaining crumbs, egg, buttermilk, baking soda, and salt. Mix thouroughly. Pour into a greased 9" x 9" pan. Sprinkle crumbs that were set aside on top.   Shake cinnamon and sugar over the top. Bake for 35 minutes.

Serves 8.

Earthquake Cake

Mary Frances Hamm and Pat Morrow of Raleigh, friends of my daughter, Jess, both recommend this fun recipe. So goooooood!

1 1/2	cups chopped pecans
1	bag (3 ounces) flaked coconut
1	German chocolate cake mix (and ingredients shown on box to prepare)
1	package (8 ounces) cream cheese, softened
1	stick butter or margarine, softened
1	box confectioners sugar

Preheat oven to 350 degrees.

Spread nuts in a greased, floured 13" x 9" pan. Spread coconut over the top of the nuts. Prepare cake mix as directed on package and pour over the coconut.

Mix cream cheese with the butter. Add sugar. Blend well and pour over cake mixture. Bake for 40 minutes.

When you take the cake out of the oven, it will be cracked on top and look like an earthquake!

Serves 8 to 10.

Fruit Cake

This is an old family recipe for a 5 pound fruit cake that would make the Claxton Bakery envious!

1/4	pound citron
1/4	pound candied lemon peel
1/4	pound candied orange peel
1/2	pound candied pineapple
1/2	pound candied cherries
6	tablespoons brandy
1/2	cup butter or margaine, softened
1/2	cup sugar
1/2	cup honey
3	eggs
2	cups all-purpose flour
1	teaspoon allspice
1/2	teaspoon nutmeg
1/2	teaspoon cloves
1	teaspoon salt
1	teaspoon baking powder
1	pound chopped pecans
1/2	pound dates
1/2	pound white raisins

Cut up citron, lemon peel, orange peel, pineapple and cherries. Soak overnight in the brandy.

Preheat oven to 250 degrees.

Cream butter and sugar well, then add the honey. Blend well. Add eggs, one at a time, beating thoroughly. Stir in flour, allspice, nutmeg, cloves, salt, and baking powder, blending well. Add pecans, dates and raisins. Pour batter over the fruit and stir together. Pour mixture into a greased and floured 10-inch tube pan.

Place the pan in the oven with a flat pan of water under the cake pan. Bake for 4 hours.

Serves 10 to 12.

Japanese Fruit Cake

*My grandmother, Liza Wooten, made this over 60 years ago.
She'd say it improved with age if just given the chance!*

1	cup butter or margarine
2	cups sugar
6	eggs, separated
3	cups all-purpose flour
4	teaspoons baking powder
2	teaspoons cinnamon
1	teaspoon cloves
1	teaspoon nutmeg
1	cup milk
1	box (15 ounces) seedless raisins
1	can (3 1/3 ounces) coconut
1	cup chopped pecans

Filling:

2	cups sugar
4	tablespoons all-purpose flour
2	lemons
2	oranges
1	bag (7 ounces) coconut

Preheat oven to 350 degrees.

Cream butter and sugar together thoroughly. Add egg yolks, one at a time, beating constantly. Sift flour, baking powder, cinnamon, cloves, and nutmeg together. Add to butter mixture alternately with the milk, blending well. Beat egg whites until stiff. Fold into the cake mixture. Pour into 4 greased and floured 8" cake pans. Bake for 30 minutes. Cool.

While the cake is cooling, prepare the filling. Squeeze juices from the lemons and oranges and set aside. Scoop out the pulp and cut into small bits. Combine the sugar, flour, and lemon and orange juices and pulp in a saucepan. Cook over medium heat until mixture thickens like honey. Add coconut and cook 2 more minutes. Spread the filling between each layer of the cake and on top.

Serves 8 to 10.

Lemon Sponge Cake

This is a really unique dessert. A lemon custard will form on the bottom with sponge cake on the top.

2	tablespoons butter or margarine
1	cup sugar
4	tablespoons all-purpose flour
3	eggs, separated
1/4	teaspoon salt
5	tablespoons lemon juice
	grated rind of 1 lemon
1 1/2	cups milk

Preheat oven to 350 degrees.

Cream butter and sugar well. Add sugar, flour, salt, lemon juice, and rind. Beat egg yolks well. Combine the eggs with the milk, then add to the butter mixture. Beat the egg whites until stiff. Fold into the cake mixture.

Pour into a greased 2-quart baking dish. Set baking dish into a pan of water. Bake for 1 hour.

Serves 6 to 8.

Lemon Pound Cake

This freezes well (wait to sift the sugar after you remove it from the freezer).

1 1/2	cups cake flour
1	teaspoon baking powder
1/2	teaspoon salt
1 1/3	sticks butter or margarine, softened
1 1/4	cups sugar
3	eggs
1/2	cup milk
1	teaspoon grated lemon rind
1	tablespoon lemon juice
	confectioners sugar

Preheat oven to 350 degrees.

Sift flour, baking powder, and salt onto wax paper. Combine butter, sugar, and eggs in a large mixing bowl. Beat with an electric mixer at high speed for 3 minutes.

Combine milk, lemon rind, and lemon juice in a cup. Stir flour mixture into batter alternately with milk mixture. Beat well by hand after each addition until smooth.

Pour batter into a greased and floured bundt or tube pan. Bake for 1 hour or until a toothpick inserted in the center comes out clean. Cool for 10 minutes before removing from pan. When completely cool, sift confectioners sugar lightly over the top of the cake.

Serves 8.

Praline Pound Cake

Rich and delicious.

1	cup butter, room temperature
1/2	cup shortening
1	package (16 ounces) dark brown sugar
5	eggs
3	cups all-purpose flour
1/2	teaspoon baking powder
1/4	teaspoon baking soda
3/4	cup milk
2	cups chopped pecans
2	teaspoons vanilla

Cream butter and shortening. Gradually add sugar and beat until light and fluffy. Add eggs, one at a time, beating well after each addition. Combine 2 1/2 cups flour, baking powder, and baking soda, stirring well. Add to creamed mixture alternately with milk. Dredge pecans in remaining 1/2 cup flour. Stir pecans and vanilla into batter.

Pour mixture into a greased and floured 10-inch tube pan. Bake for 1 1/4 hours or until toothpick inserted in center comes out clean. Cool in the pan for 10 minutes, then remove from pan to continue cooling.

Serves 8 to 10.

Pineapple Cake

My good friend and chef, Cora Davis, at the Kinston Country Club made this often.

1	stick butter or margarine
2	cups sugar
5	eggs
1	box (14 ounces) graham cracker crumbs
1	teaspoon baking powder
1	cup milk
2	teaspoons vanilla
1	cup chopped pecans
1	cup coconut

Icing:

1/2	stick butter or margarine
1/2	box confectioners sugar
1	cup crushed pineapple, drained

Preheat oven to 350 degrees.

Cream butter and sugar well. Beat eggs well, then add to the butter mixture. Add graham cracker crumbs and baking powder. Gradually add milk and mix well. Add vanilla, pecans, and coconut, mixing well.

Pour batter into a greased and floured tube pan. Bake for 1 hour.

While cake is cooking, prepare the icing. Melt butter in a saucepan. Add sugar and pineapple. Bring to a boil, stirring constantly. Spoon over cake while cake is still hot.

Serves 8.

Prune Cake

One of the best spice cakes ever.

1 1/2	cups sugar
1	cup vegetable oil
3	eggs
2	cups all-purpose flour
1	teaspoon baking soda
1	teaspoon nutmeg
1	teaspoon allspice
1	teaspoon cinnamon
1	cup buttermilk
1	cup prunes cooked and chopped
1	cup chopped pecans
1/2	teaspoon salt

Icing:

1	cup sugar
1/2	cup buttermilk
1/2	teaspoon baking soda
1	tablespoon corn syrup
1/2	stick butter or margarine
1/2	teaspoon vanilla

Combine sugar and oil in a mixing bowl and blend well. Add eggs one at a time, mixing after each addition. Combine flour, baking soda, nutmeg, allspice, and cinnamon and add to egg mixture alternately with milk. Add prunes and pecans, mixing well.

Pour into a greased and floured bundt pan. Bake for 55 minutes.

While cake is cooking, prepare icing. Combine sugar, baking soda, corn syrup, butter and vanilla in a saucepan. Bring to a boil, stirring constantly. Boil until mixture forms a soft boil (on a candy thermometer). Pour icing over the cake while the cake is still hot.

Serves 8 to 10.

Sponge Cake

Serve with fresh strawberries and whipped cream for a delicious strawberry shortcake

4	**eggs, separated**
1/2	**teaspoon salt**
1 1/2	**cups sugar**
1	**teaspoon vanilla**
1 1/2	**cups all-purpose flour**
1/2	**teaspoon cream of tartar**

Preheat oven to 350 degrees.

Beat egg yolks and 1/4 teaspoon salt until mixture is very thick. Add 2 tablespoons of cold water. Beat 1 minute, then add 1/2 cup hot water. Heat mixture for about 5 minutes. Gradually beat in sugar. Add vanilla and beat until mixture is very fluffy. Blend in flour.

Beat egg whites until frothy. Add cream of tartar and 1/4 teaspoon salt, then beat until egg whites are stiff. Fold whites into egg yolk mixture. Pour batter into an ungreased 10-inch tube pan. Bake for 1 hour. Invert pan on cake cooler or glass. Let cake cool for 20 minutes, then cut cake away from pan with a sharp knife. Place cake on a rack to continue cooling.

Serves 8 to 10.

Tipsey Cake

A favorite of my family and always requested at our Christmas day dinner.

1	medium sized (14 to 16 ounces) angel food cake
1/2	cup burgundy wine or to taste
1	package (6 ounces) vanilla pudding mix
2	cups milk
1	pint whipping cream
1	cup bourbon whiskey
1	package (2 ounces) slivered almonds, toasted
1	jar (6 ounces) cherries with stems

Break cake into bite size pieces. Place 1/3 of the cake into a serving bowl (I use a 2-quart silver bowl). Sprinkle wine over the first layer of cake.

Prepare pudding mix with milk according to package directions.

Whip cream until thickened. Slowly add 1/2 cup of bourbon. Whip until peaks form.

Place 1/3 of the custard mixture over the first layer of cake. Cover this with 1/3 of the whipping cream. Place another layer of 1/3 of the cake. Cover this layer with 1/3 of the custard mixture. Add a layer of 1/3 of the whipping cream. Place the remaining cake as the next layer. Sprinkle this layer with the remaining 1/2 cup of bourbon. Add the remaining custard mixture as the next layer. Frost the top with the remaining whipped cream.

Top with almonds and cherries.

Serves 8 to 10.

Caramel Icing

This recipe came from the best cook I've known, my mother-in-law, Amine Galbreath, and it's a favorite of our whole family.

1 1/2	cups dark brown sugar
1	stick butter
1	cup evaporated milk
3	cups confectioners (4 X) sugar, sifted
1 1/2	teaspoons vanilla
	pinch salt

Combine sugar, butter and milk in a saucepan. Bring to a boil and continue to boil for 5 to 6 minutes, stirring constantly. Place sifted confectioners sugar in a mixing bowl. Slowly add milk mixture, beating well with an electric mixer. Add vanilla and salt. Continue beating until mixture is smooth and creamy.

Spread over the cake of your choice.

Makes enough icing for a 2-layer cake.

Apple Streusel Cobbler

Eat this warm with ice cream or serve after it has cooled. Either way you'll have a winner!

2	cans (21 ounces each) apple pie filling
2	eggs
1	can sweetened condensed milk
1/2	cup butter or margarine
1/2	teaspoon cinnamon
1/4	teaspoon nutmeg
1/2	cup firmly packed light brown sugar
1/2	cup all-purpose flour
1/2	cup chopped pecans
1/2	cup oatmeal

Preheat oven to 375 degrees.

Spread apple pie filling in a buttered 9-inch square baking pan. Place eggs in a medium mixing bowl and beat well. Add milk, 1/4 cup melted butter, cinnamon and nutmeg and mix well. Pour egg mixture over the pie filling.

Combine sugar and flour in a mixing bowl. Cut in remaining 1/4 cup of butter with a fork until mixture is crumbly. Add nuts and oatmeal. Sprinkle over top. Bake for 50 to 55 minutes or until set.

Refrigerate leftovers.

Serves 8 to 10.

Apple Crisp

I recommend using either Rome or Granny Smith apples.

6	**cups peeled and sliced cooking apples**
2	**tablespoons sugar**
1/2	**teaspoon cinnamon**
1	**cup all-purpose flour**
1	**cup firmly packed brown sugar**
1	**cup butter or margarine, melted**
1/2	**cup quick cooking oatmeal, uncooked**

Preheat oven to 350 degrees.

Place apples in a 9" x 13 " baking dish. Sprinkle with sugar and cinnamon. Combine flour, sugar, butter and oatmeal in a bowl, mixing well. Pour over apples.

Bake for 30 minutes or until apples are tender.

Serves 6.

Blueberry-Peach Crisp

It's hard to wait until blueberry season for this one.

3   cups fresh blueberries (can substitute blackberries)
6   cups sliced fresh peaches
1/2   cup brown sugar
2   tablespoons all-purpose flour
1   tablespoon plus 2 teaspoons cinnamon
1   cup quick cooking oatmeal, uncooked
3   tablespoons butter or margarine, softened
       whipped cream or vanilla ice cream

Preheat oven to 350 degrees.

Combine blueberries and peaches in a 1-quart baking dish. Combine 1/4 cup sugar, flour and 1 tablespoon cinnamon in a small mixing bowl, then toss with fruit.

Combine oatmeal, 1/4 cup sugar and 2 teaspoons cinnamon in a small mixing bowl. Cut in butter until mixture is crumbly. Sprinkle over the fruit.

Bake for 25 minutes. Mixture should be bubbling and fruit still firm. Serve hot or cold. Garnish with whipped cream or ice cream.

Serves 6 to 8.

Fresh Fruit Cobbler

Children of all ages love this one.

1/4   cup butter or margarine, softened
2/3   cup sugar
1   cup all-purpose flour
2   teaspoons baking powder
1/4   teaspoon salt
1/2   cup milk
3   cups fresh fruit (blueberries, blackberries, or sliced
      peaches)
1   cup orange juice
      ice cream

Preheat oven to 375 degrees.

Cream butter and 1/3 cup sugar together until fluffy. Add flour, baking powder, and salt alternately with milk. Mix until smooth. Pour into a 9" by 9" baking pan.

Toss fruit with 1/3 cup sugar, then spoon over batter. Pour orange juice over the top.

Bake for 45 to 50 minutes. Batter will form a cakelike layer over fruit while baking. Serve warm with ice cream.

Serve 8.

Easy to Make Fruit Cobbler

This "never fail" cobbler recipe was passed from Brenda Stewart of Cary (NC) to my daughter, then to me.

1	can (20 ounces) crushed pineapple
1	can (20 ounces) fruit pie filling (apple, cherry, peach or other fruit of your choice)
1	box yellow cake mix
2	sticks butter or margarine
1	cup chopped pecans

Preheat oven to 350 degrees.

Lightly grease a 13" x 9" baking pan. Spread undrained pineapple over the bottom of the pan. Add layer of fruit pie filling. Sprinkle the dry cake mix evenly over the fruit. Dot the butter over the cake mix. Sprinkle nuts on top.

Bake for 25 minutes. Remove the cobbler from the oven and cut down to the bottom of the pan to let the juices rise. Return to the oven and bake for 10 to 15 minutes more. Serve hot with ice cream.

Serves 6 to 8.

Bread Pudding

My grandmother, Liza Wooten of Kinston, perfected this favorite over the years with loving care.

3	**cups small white bread cubes**
2	**cups milk**
1/2	**stick butter or margarine**
1/2	**cup sugar**
3	**eggs, beaten**
3	**bananas, chopped**
1	**large Rome apple, peeled and chopped**
1	**cup raisins**
1	**teaspoon vanilla**

Hard Sauce:

1	**cup sugar**
1/2	**stick butter or margarine**
1	**teaspoon vanilla**

Preheat oven to 350 degrees.

Combine bread cubes and milk and set aside.

Cream sugar and butter in a mixing bowl until smooth. Add eggs and mix well. Mix in soaked bread. Add bananas, apple, raisins, and vanilla. Place mixture in a 9" x 9" greased baking pan. Bake for 30 minutes.

While pudding is baking, prepare the hard sauce. Cream butter and sugar until smooth. Add vanilla. Serve over hot pudding.

Serves 6 to 8.

Frozen Lemon Pudding

Amine Galbreath of Kinston, my mother-in-law, served this often.

4	tablespoons lemon juice
3	eggs, separated
1/2	cup sugar
	grated rind of 1 lemon
1/2	pint whipping cream, whipped
1/2	cup graham cracker crumbs

Combine lemon juice, egg yolks, sugar, and lemon rind in the top of a double boiler. Cook until smooth and thickened, stirring constantly. Cool. Fold stiffly beaten eggs whites and whipped cream into the lemon mixture.

Sprinkle graham cracker crumbs in a 9" x 9" baking pan. Pour in lemon mixture. Freeze until firm. Cut into squares to serve.

Serves 8 to 10.

Rice Pudding

My grandmother, Liza Wooten of Kinston (NC) perfected this one, too.

1/2	cup regular long-grain rice
2	cups milk
1/2	pint heavy cream
3	large eggs, separated
1/3	cup sugar
1	teaspoon vanilla
1/8	teaspoon salt
1/8	teaspoon nutmeg
1/4	cup seedless raisins

Heat 1 cup water and rice in a heavy 2-quart saucepan over medium heat. Bring to a boil, then reduce heat to low. Cover and cook for 15 minutes or until rice is tender, but firm. Add milk and cream and heat to boiling over medium heat. Reduce heat to low. Cover and simmer 20 minutes or until rice is very tender, strring frequently to avoid scorching.

While rice is cooking, butter 6 10-ounce custard cups. When rice is tender, remove from heat. Beat egg yolks in a small bowl. Add a small amount of hot rice mixture into the beaten eggs. Stir egg mixture into the remaining rice in the saucepan. Stir in sugar, vanilla, salt, and nutmeg. Cool slightly.

Preheat oven to 350 degrees.

Divide raisins among cups. Beat egg whites in a bowl until stiff. Gently fold in rice mixture with a rubber spatula.

Place a large roasting pan with 1/2 inch hot water in the oven. Spoon rice mixture into the cups. Place the cups in the roasting pan.

Bake for 25 to 30 minutes or until golden brown. Carefully remove the cups from the pan and cool on a wire rack. Cover each cup and refrigerate until cold.

Serves 6.

Chocolate Mousse

This can be frozen.

3	eggs, separated
1 1/2	teaspoons vanilla
1/2	teaspoon almond extract
4	squares (1-ounce each) semisweet chocolate, melted
1/2	teaspoon cream of tartar
1/2	cup sugar
1	cup whipping cream

Beat egg yolks slightly. Add vanilla, almond extract, and chocolate to egg yolks, stirring well.

Beat eggs whites and cream of tartar until frothy. Gradually add sugar, beating 2 to 4 minutes until stiff peaks form. Stir about 1/4 of the egg white mixture into the chocolate mixture. Fold remaining egg mixture into the chocolate mixture.

Beat whipping cream until soft peaks form. Fold cream into the chocolate mixture. Cover and chill at least 2 hours.

Serves 6 to 8.

Chocolate Charlotte Russe

This takes a little time but you'll be glad you made the extra effort.

2	**envelopes plain gelatin**
8	**ounces bitter chocolate**
6	**eggs, separated**
1 1/2	**cups sugar**
	dash of salt
1	**teaspoon vanilla**
1/2	**teaspoon cream of tartar**
1/2	**cup chopped pecans**
2	**dozen lady fingers**
2	**cups heavy whipping cream**

Soften gelatin in 4 tablespoons cold water. Combine chocolate and 1 cup of water in a saucepan. Heat over low heat, stirring constantly, until the chocolate melts. Remove from heat. Add gelatine, stirring well.

Beat egg yolks until thick. Gradually add 1 cup of sugar. Add salt and vanilla. Combine chocolate mixture with egg yolks. Cool.

Beat egg whites with cream of tartar until peaks form. Gradually add 1/2 cup sugar. Fold into chocolate mixture.

Beat whipping cream until stiff. Fold in half of the whipped cream into the chocolate mixture. Add the pecans.

Split the lady fingers and line a springform pan with half of them. Pour in half of the chocolate mixture. Crumble remaining lady fingers over chocolate mixture, then spoon the remaining chocolate mixture on top. Top chocolate with remaining whipped cream. Shave bits of chocolate on top. Refrigerate several hours until set.

Serves 8.

Lemon Bisque

Light and lucious.

1	can (13 ounces) evaporated milk
1	package (3 ounces) lemon jello
1/2	cup sugar
	dash of salt
5	tablespoons lemon juice
	grated rind of 1 lemon
2 1/2	cups graham or cinnamon crisp cracker crumbs
	slivered almonds
	whipped cream

Place milk in a bowl in the freezer until the milk starts to freeze. Combine jello, 1 1/4 cups boiling water, sugar and salt in a bowl. Stir until jello is dissolved. Cool, then add lemon juice and lemon rind.

Remove milk from the freezer and whip until stiff and double in bulk. Fold milk into the jello mixture.

Line a 9" x 13" pan with cracker crumbs. Spoon jello mixture into the pan. Sprinkle almonds on top. Refrigerate for several hours until firm. Cut into squares and serve with whipped cream.

Serves 8 to 10.

Caramel Flan

A light dessert for custard lovers.

1 1/4	**cups sugar**
2	**cups milk**
2	**cups light cream**
6	**eggs**
1/2	**teaspoon salt**
2	**teaspoons vanilla**

Preheat oven to 325 degrees.

Place 3/4 cup sugar in a large, heavy skillet. Cook over medium heat until sugar melts and forms a light brown syrup. Stir to blend.

Pour syrup into individual custard cups, covering bottom and sides completely. Set aside.

Heat milk and cream in a saucepan until bubbles form around the edge of the pan.

Beat eggs in a large bowl. Add 1/2 cup sugar, salt, and vanilla. Gradually add hot milk mixture, stirring well. Pour into the prepared custard cups.

Bake for 45 minutes. Let custard cool. Refrigerate for 2 to 3 hours or overnight.To serve, loosen custard from cups using a small spatula. Invert the cup onto a serving plate. Gently shake to release.

Serves 8.

Dirt Dessert

This is a fun dessert for both kids and adults. You can be really creative in your decorating to enhance the "dirt" look.

1/2	stick butter or margarine, softened
1	package (8 ounces) cream cheese
1	cup confectioners sugar
3 1/2	cups milk
2	packages (3 1/2 ounces each) instant vanilla pudding mix
1	container (12 ounces) frozen whipped topping, thawed
2	packages (20 ounces each) Oreo cookies, crushed in a plastic bag with a rolling pin

Cream butter, cream cheese, and confectioners sugar in a mixing bowl until smooth.

In another bowl, combine milk, pudding mix, and whipped topping. Add butter mixture and blend well.

Put 1/3 of the crushed cookies in the bottom of a plastic sand pail or flower pot (approximately 2-quart size) or a 9" x 13" baking pan. Add 1/2 of the pudding mixture. Top with 1/3 of the cookies, then 1/2 of the pudding mixture. Top with remaining crushed cookies.

Stick artifical flowers in the center and add gummy worms on top. You have a "beautiful" dirt dessert!

Makes 12 servings.

Ambrosia

Food of the gods!

3   **cups orange sections**
1   **cup freshly grated coconut**
2   **tablespoons sugar**
1/2   **cup whipping cream, whipped**
2   **tablespoons confectioners sugar**

Combine orange sections, coconut, and sugar. Combine whipped cream and confectioners sugar, then fold into the fruit mixture. Refrigerate until ready to serve.

Serves 4 to 6.

Champagne Fruit

A truly elegant dessert.

1	box (10 ounces) frozen strawberries
1	box (10 ounces) frozen peaches
1	box (10 ounces) frozen raspberries
1	can (8 ounces) pineapple chunks, chilled
1/2	cup brandy
1	bottle (fifth) champagne, chilled

Place all partially thawed fruit in a bowl. Pour brandy over the fruit, stirring well. Let stand in the refrigerator for 4 hours. When ready to serve, spoon fruit halfway to top of chilled champagne glasses. Pour enough champagne over fruit to fill glass.

Serves 10.

Heavenly Hash

A heavenly dessert!

1	large can (20 ounces) crushed pineapple
3	cups miniature marshmallows
1	cup chopped pecans
1	small jar (6 ounces) cherries, cut in half
1	pint heavy whipping cream, whipped
1	teaspoon vanilla

Combine pinapple, marshmallows, pecans, and cherries. Combine whipped cream and vanilla and fold into pinapple mixture. Chill thoroughly. Serve in individual compotes.

Serves 6 to 8.

Prune Elegante

For the best flavor, prepare this recipe three days before you are ready to serve.

1	**package (8 ounces) pitted prunes**
1	**bottle port wine**
3/4	**cup sugar**
1	**teaspoon vanilla**
1	**cup whipping cream, whipped**

Place prunes in a shallow glass baking dish. Cover with wine. Cover dish and place in the refrigerator for 48 hours.

Remove prunes from the refrigerator and place in a large saucepan. Add sugar and vanilla. bring to a boil, then reduce heat and simmer for 10 minutes. Remove from heat. Cover mixture with additional wine and marinate in the refrigerator for 24 more hours.

To serve, spoon into dessert dishes and garnish with whipped cream.

Serves 6.

Chocolate Ice Cream

A favorite of young and old alike.

5	squares (1-ounce) unsweetened chocolate, melted
1	can sweetened condensed milk
4	egg yolks
2	teaspoons vanilla
2	cups light cream
2	cups heavy whipping cream
1	cup chopped pecans

Beat melted chocolate, milk, egg yolks, and vanilla in a large bowl. Stir in light cream, heavy cream and nuts. Pour into an ice cream freezer container. Freeze according to manufacturer's directions. Store leftovers in the freezer.

Makes 1 1/2 quarts.

Vanilla Ice Cream

This basic recipe can also be used to make peach or banana ice cream.

4	**eggs, separated**
1	**cup sugar**
2	**tablespoons all-purpose flour**
2	**teaspoons vanilla**
	dash of salt
1	**quart whole milk**
1	**pint heavy whipping cream**

Slightly beat egg yolks in a small bowl. Gradually add sugar, beating constantly. Blend in flour.

Place milk in a large saucepan. Slowly add egg mixture. Heat to a boil, then reduce heat and simmer until thickened like a custard. Stir in vanilla and salt. Cool.

Whip egg whites until stiff. Whip cream until soft peaks form. Fold egg whites and cream into the custard. Pour into an ice cream freezer container. Freeze according to manufacturer's directions. Store leftovers in the freezer.

Makes 2 quarts.

To make peach ice cream, add 2 to 3 pounds of peeled and mashed peaches to the custard before placing in the ice cream freezer.

To make banana ice cream, add 4 to 5 mashed bananas to the custard before placing in the ice cream freezer.

Caramel Sauce

Serve this sauce over vanilla ice cream. You can store it for up to 2 weeks in the refrigerator.

1 1/2	**cups packed brown sugar**
1	**tablespoon cornstarch**
1	**cup half and half**
2	**tablespoons butter or margarine**

Combine brown sugar and cornstarch in a medium saucepan. Add half and half and butter. Cook until mixture boils, stirring constantly. Reduce heat and simmer for 8 to 10 minutes, stirring occassionally until mixture thickens.

Makes 1 3/4 cups.

Chocolate Fudge Sauce

This really is the "best I ever tasted." It's good enough to eat by itself, but you really should serve it over ice cream.

1	bar (8 ounces) unsweetened chocolate
1	bar (8 ounces) semisweet chocolate
1	can (14 ounces) sweetened condensed milk
1	can (12 ounces) evaporated milk
1/2	cup confectioners sugar
2	teaspoons vanilla

Melt chocolate and milk in a saucepan over low heat, stirring frequently. When chocolate is melted, remove from heat and stir in sugar and vanilla.

May be stored in the refrigerator for up to 2 weeks. If the sauce is too thick when removed from the refrigerator, add a little milk and stir until smooth. Serve hot (microwave about 1 1/2 minutes) or cold.

Makes 4 cups.

Chocolate Bourbon Candy

Make early and serve during the holiday season.

1/2	cup plus 1 teaspoon butter or margarine, softened
3	tablespoons sweetened condensed milk
1/3	cup plus 2 teaspoons bourbon
7 1/2	cups confectioners sugar, sifted
1/2	cup finely chopped pecans
1	package (12 ounces) chocolate chips
72	pecan halves

Mix 1/2 cup butter, milk and bourbon. Add sugar and knead until mixture doesn't stick to your hands. Knead in chopped pecans, then shape into 1-inch (or smaller) balls.

Combine chocolate chips and 1 teaspoon butter in the top of a double boiler. Cook until chocolate is melted and well blended with the butter.

Dip balls into the melted chocolate, using a toothpick. Place on waxed paper, remove the toothpick, and press a pecan half on each piece. Allow chocolate to cool and harden before storing in an airtight container.

Makes 6 dozen.

Fudge

I've made this for years - it's a winner!

2/3   **cup cocoa**
3   **cups sugar**
1/8   **teaspoon salt**
1 1/2   **cups milk**
1/4   **cup butter or margarine**
1   **teaspoon vanilla**

Combine cocoa, sugar, and salt in a heavy 4-quart pan. Stir in milk. Bring to a boil, stirring constantly. Boil to soft ball stage (238° on a candy thermometer). Remove from heat and add butter and vanilla. **Do not stir.**

Cool at room temperature to 110°. Beat until fudge thickens and looses some of its gloss. Quickly spread in a lightly buttered 9" x 9" pan. Cool.

Makes 36 squares.

Peanut Brittle

Nice and crunchy.

2	**cups sugar**
1	**cup light corn syrup**
1/2	**teaspoon salt**
4	**cups raw, shelled peanuts, skins on**
2	**tablespoons butter**
1	**teaspoon baking soda**

Heat sugar, syrup, 1/2 cup water, and salt in a heavy saucepan. Bring to a rolling boil. Add peanuts. Reduce heat to medium and cook until syrup spins a thread (293°), stirring constantly.

Add butter, then baking soda. Beat rapidly and pour on a buttered surface, spreading to 1/4-inch thickness. When cool, break into pieces.

Makes about 1 pound.

Bourbon Balls

An old Kentucky recipe.

3	**cups vanilla wafer crumbs**
1/2	**cup finely chopped pecans**
1/2	**cup powdered cocoa**
2	**cups confectioners sugar**
1/2	**cup bourbon (may substitute rum)**
3	**tablespoons light corn syrup**
	dash of salt

Blend together crumbs, pecans, cocoa, 1 cup of confectioners sugar, bourbon, corn syrup and salt. Form in small balls, approximately 1-inch in size.

Roll each ball in the remaining confectioners sugar and place on a cookie sheet. Chill in the refrigerator for several hours or overnight.

Makes 3 dozen.

Buckeye Candy

Another holiday treat.

3	packages (1 pound each) confectioners sugar
2	pounds chunky peanut butter
3	tablespoons vanilla
1	pound butter
2	packages (12 ounces each) semi-sweet chocolate bits
1/2	bar parafin

Combine sugar, peanut butter, vanilla, and butter and knead until sugar is blended thoroughly. Mixture wil be a dough-like consistency. Form into balls the size of a small buckeye.

Melt chocolate bits with parafin in a double boiler. Dip the balls into the chocolate, using a toothpick (cover the sides and leave the top to look like a buckeye).

Makes 6 pounds.

Chocolate Truffles

Use finely chopped almonds to roll half of the balls for variety.

2/3	**cup heavy whipping cream**
3	**tablepsoons butter or margarine**
2	**tablespoons sugar**
1	**tablespoon almond liqueur (may use your choice)**
2	**packages (4 ounces each) German sweet chocolate, broken into bits**
1	**cup finely chopped pecans**

Combine cream, butter, and sugar in a saucepan. Bring to a full boil over medium heat, stirring constantly. Remove from heat.

Add liqueur and chocolate. Stir until the chocolate melts and the mixture is smooth. Cover and place in the the refrigerator for 3 1/2 hours or until mixture is firm enough to handle.

Remove from the refrigerator and shape into 1-inch balls. Roll in the pecans. Store in the refrigerator.

Makes 2 dozen.

Date Nut Balls

Always a favorite.

1/2	cup butter or margarine
3/4	cup sugar
1	package (8 ounces) dates, chopped
2 1/2	cups crisp rice cereal
1	cup chopped pecans
	confectioners sugar

Combine butter, sugar, and dates in a medium saucepan. Bring to a boil. Cook for 3 minutes, stirring constantly. Stir in cereal and pecans. Cool to touch.

Shape into 1-inch balls and roll each in confectioners sugar.

Make 4 dozen.

Christmas Nut Thins

Fill a tin full to make a nice gift at Christmas.

1	cup butter or margarine, softened
1	cup sugar
2	eggs, well beaten
1 1/2	cups all-purpose flour
1/2	teaspoon salt
1	cup chopped pecans
1	teaspoon vanilla
	pecan halves

Preheat oven to 375 degrees.

Cream butter and sugar until smooth. Add eggs, beating well. Add flour and salt and mix until smooth. Stir in chopped pecans and vanilla, mixing well.

Drop dough by 1/2 teaspoonfuls about an inch apart on a greased cookie sheet. Place a pecan half in the center of each cookie. Bake about 8 minutes or until lightly browned.

Makes 6 dozen.

Pecan Crescents

Keep on hand for afternoon tea!

---

2   **cups all-purpose flour**
2   **cups chopped pecans**
1/4   **cup sugar**
1   **cup butter or margarine, melted**
2   **teaspoons vanilla**
       confectioners sugar

Preheat oven to 325 degrees.

Combine flour, pecans, sugar, butter, and vanilla, mixing well (dough will be slightly crumbly). Shape dough into crescents. Place on an ungreased cookie sheet.

Bake for 18 to 20 minutes or until golden. Cool on wire racks and sprinkle with confectioners sugar.

Makes 3 dozen.

Pecan Pralines

Sweet and wonderful.

1	package (1 pound) brown sugar
1	can (6 ounces) evaporated milk
1	tablespoon butter or margarine
	pinch of salt
1	teaspoon vanilla
1	cup chopped pecans

Combine sugar, milk, butter and salt in a saucepan. Cook to a soft ball stage (238^0 on a candy thermometer). Cool for a few minutes, then add vanilla and beat by hand until creamy, about 2 minutes. Add pecans and beat until mixture looses the glossy look.

Drop by heaping tablespoonfuls on a greased cookie sheet. Add a teaspoon or so of hot water if pralines get too hard to drop.

Makes 30.

Saltine Cookies

Surprisingly good.

1 1/2	**sticks butter or margarine**
1	**cup brown sugar**
40	**saltine crackers**
1	**package (12 ounces) chocolate chips**
1	**cup chopped pecans**

Preheat oven to 350 degrees.

Melt butter in a saucepan. Add the brown sugar and cook until foamy.

Place crackers side by side on 11" x 16" cookie sheet with a non-stick coating, completely filling the surface. If bottom row of crackers will not fit, trim them with scissors. Crackers must fit tightly.

Pour the butter mixture evenly over the crackers. Bake for 10 minutes. Remove from oven and immediately spread chocolate chips over the crackers. Sprinkle pecans over the melted chocolate, then lightly mash the pecans into the chocolate.

Cool and break into pieces.

Makes 40.

From Scratch Brownies

If you really want to impress your guests, you can make your brownies "from scratch."

3	**squares (1 ounce each) unsweetened chocolate, chopped**
1/2	**cup butter or margarine, cut up**
1	**cup sugar**
2	**eggs**
1/2	**teaspoon vanilla**
1/2	**cup all-purpose flour**
1/4	**teaspoon salt**
1	**cup chopped pecans**

Preheat oven to 325 degrees.

Combine chocolate and butter in a saucepan. Cook over low heat until chocolate is melted. Stir in sugar. Mix well, then add eggs and vanilla. Beat until well combined. Stir in flour and salt. Fold in pecans.

Pour into a greased and floured 8" x 8" pan. Bake for 40 minutes or until center is just set. Cool completely on a wire rack. Cut into 2 inch squares.

Makes 16.

Crumbly Bars

This is another favorite shared by my mother-in-law, Amine Galbreath. These are easy to make but look like you spent hours!

1/2	cup butter or margarine
1	cup sugar
2	cups self-rising flour
1	teaspoon cinnamon
1	teaspoon allspice
1/2	cup dates, chopped
1	egg
1/2	cup milk
1	teaspoon vanilla
1/2	teaspoon almond extract
1/2	cups chopped pecans
1/4	cup citron
1/4	cup lemon or orange peel
	confectioners sugar

Preheat oven to 350 degrees.

Combine butter, sugar, flour, cinnamon, and allspice in a mixing bowl and blend well. Remove 2/3 cup of this mixture and set aside.

Add egg to the remaining mixture and blend well. Blend in milk, vanilla, almond extract, pecans, citron, and lemon peel. Pour batter into a greased and floured 9" x 13" pan. Cover with reserved sugar mixture. Bake for 25 minutes. Cool slightly. Cut into bars and roll each bar in confectioners sugar.

Makes 16 to 20.

Date Nut Bars

My mother, Helen Jones of Greenville (NC), made these often.

5	eggs, separated
1	cup sugar
1	cup all-purpose flour
2	tablespoons baking powder
1	cup chopped dates
1	cup chopped pecans
	confectioners sugar

Preheat oven to 325 degrees.

Beat egg yolks until light. Add sugar gradually and beat until creamy. Add dates and pecans. Mix well so that dates and pecans are well coated and separated. Sift in flour and baking powder and mix well. Beat egg whites until stiff, then add to date mixture.

Pour batter into a greased and floured 9" x 13" pan. Bake for 30 minutes. Cool and cut into bars. Roll in confectioners sugar.

Makes 16 to 20.

Lemon Bars

Mimi Parrott of Salisbury (NC) shared this one. This is tangy and sweet.

First layer:

2	cups all-purpose flour
1/2	cup confectioners sugar (4X)
1	cup butter or margarine

Second layer:

4	eggs, beaten
2	cups sugar
1/3	cup lemon juice
1/4	cup all-purpose flour
1/2	teaspoon baking powder
	confectioners sugar

Preheat oven to 350 degrees.

Prepare the first layer by sifting together the flour and sugar. Cut in the butter until the mixture clings together. Press into a 9" x 13" pan. Bake for 20 to 25 minutes.

While first layer is cooking, prepare the second layer. Combine eggs, sugar, and lemon juice. Sift together flour and baking powder and beat into egg mixture. Remove first layer from the oven and spread second layer over the top. Bake for 25 additional minutes. Cool. Sprinkle with confectioners sugar and cut into bars.

Makes 16 to 20.

Pecan Tassies

Kathleen Ward, originally from Kinston (NC), made these often. They are great for parties.

Pastry:
1	package (3 ounces) cream cheese
1/2	cup butter
1	cup all-purpose flour

Filling:
1	egg
3/4	cup brown sugar
1	tablespoon butter or margarine, melted
1	teaspoon vanilla
	dash of salt
3/4	cup chopped pecans

Preheat oven to 325 degrees.

Prepare the pastry by creaming the butter and cheese. Stir in the flour and mix well. Chill dough for at least 1 hour. Shape dough into 2-ounce balls. Place in ungreased miniature muffin tins. Press dough into the bottom and sides of the tins.

Prepare the filling by beating the eggs, sugar, butter, vanilla and salt together. Divide the pecans in half. Place half of the pecans on the pastry. Spoon filling into the tins up to 1/2 full. Place the remaining nuts on top of each tin. Bake for 25 minutes or until crust turns light brown. Cool in the muffin tins until set.

Makes 15 to 20.

Toffee Treats

Don't worry about the calories - just enjoy!

1	cup butter or margarine, softened
1	cup firmly packed brown sugar
1	egg yolk
1	teaspoon vanilla
2	cups all-purpose flour
1/4	teaspoon salt
5	milk chocolate bars (1.65 ounces each), broken
3/4	cup chopped pecans, toasted

Preheat oven to 350 degrees.

Cream butter and sugar until smooth. Add egg and vanilla and beat well. Mix in flour and salt.

Spread batter into a lightly greased 9" x 13" pan. Bake for 25 to 30 minutes (crust will be soft). Remove from oven and arrange pieces of chocolate bars on hot crust. Let stand until the chocolate softens, then spread chocolate evenly over the crust with a spatula. Sprinkle pecans on top. Cool slightly, then cut into squares. Let cool completely in pan.

Makes 3 dozen.

Meringue Shells

You can fill the meringues with any filling you choose, but my favorite is the lemon filling shown below.

3	**egg whites**
1/4	**teaspoon cream of tartar**
2/3	**cup sugar**

Preheat oven to 275 degrees.

Beat egg whites with cream of tartar until soft peaks are formed. Gradually add sugar, 1 tablespoon at a time. Continue beating until mixture is thick and glossy.

Drop by tablespoonfuls on a buttered cookie sheet. Make a slight depression in the middle. Bake for 1 hour. Turn off oven and let meringue cool in the oven for an additional hour. Fill with your favorite filling.

Makes 6 individual shells.

Lemon Filling

1 1/2	**cups sugar**
6	**tablespoons cornstarch**
1/2	**cup fresh lemon juice**
3	**egg yolks**
2	**tablespoons butter or margarine**
1	**teaspoon grated lemon rind**
8	**ounces heavy whipping cream, whipped**

Combine sugar and cornstarch in a saucepan over medium heat, stirring thoroughly. Stir in lemon juice.

Combine egg yolks and 1/2 cup cold water in a small bowl and blend well. Gradually stir into cornstarch mixture. Add butter. Gradually stir in 1 1/2 cups boiling water. Cook over medium heat, stirring constantly until mixture comes to a full boil. Remove from heat and stir in the lemon rind. Cover and cool. Fill meringue shells and garnish with whipped cream.

Cream Puffs

These freeze well.

1/2	cup milk
1/2	cup sifted all-purpose flour
1/4	cup butter or margarine
1/8	teaspoon salt
2	eggs

Filling:

1	cup heavy whipping cream
1	teaspoon sugar
1/2	teaspoon vanilla
	confectioners sugar (4X)

Preheat oven to 400 degrees.

Combine milk and butter in a saucepan and bring to a slow boil. Add flour and salt. Cook and stir the batter until it forms a ball, leaving the sides of the pan. Remove from heat. Beat in eggs, one at a time, blending first egg well before adding the next.

Place small teaspoonfuls of batter on a greased baking sheet about 2 inches apart. Bake for 30 minutes (if puffs are small, bake for 15 minutes). Reduce heat to 350 degrees and continue baking for 5 more minutes. Cool.

While puffs are cooling. prepare the filling. Whip cream until stiff. Gradually add sugar and vanilla and beat for 2 more minutes. Make a gash in the side of each puff and fill with filling. Shake confectioners sugar on the top of each puff.

Makes 2 dozen small or 12 large puffs.

Chocolate Dipped Strawberries

This is a great dessert or hors d'oeuvre when strawberries are juicy and sweet!

4   ounces semisweet chocolate
1   pint fresh strawberries

Break or chop chocolate coarsely. Place chocolate in a small heatproof bowl, then place bowl in a small skillet over low heat with about 1/2 inch of barely simmering water. Heat, stirring occassionally, until the chocolate is melted. Be careful that no water gets into the chocolate. Stir until smooth. Remove skillet from the heat, leaving the bowl of chocolate in the hot water.

Wash and pat the strawberries dry with paper towels. Holding by the stem, dip each strawberry in the chocolate to cover about 3/4 of the berry. Let excess chocolate drip off the berry, then place it on a tray covered with wax paper. Refrigerate to harden. Serve strawberries on a small dessert plate.

Make about 6 servings.

Index

YES! I need additional copies of *The Best I Ever Tasted* by Margaret J. Galbreath.

It's as simple as 1,2,3:

Just fill in the information below (please print), detach this page and mail to: The Roper Group, PO Box 20573, Raleigh, NC 27619 or call: (919) 782-8956.

---

❶

	# Copies Ordered	$ Subtotal
The Best I Ever Tasted @ $20.09ea. (incl. tax)	_____	$_____
Shipping 1 book $3.00 2 books $4.50 (more than 2, please call)		$_____
TOTALS	_____	$_____

---

❷

MasterCard/Visa Welcomed

Payment by:
☐ Check (Payable to The Roper Group)
☐ MasterCard/Visa

Exp. Date:_____

Card No.: _____

Signature: _____

---

❸

Name: _____

Telephone: _____

Address: _____
                                            Street

_____
        City   **State**   **Zip**